Understanding American Icons

green press INITIATIVE

Left Coast Press is committed to preserving ancient forests and natural resources. We elected to print this title on 30% post consumer recycled paper, processed chlorine free. As a result, for this printing, we have saved:

3 Trees (40' tall and 6-8" diameter)
1 Million BTUs of Total Energy
235 Pounds of Greenhouse Gases
1,059 Gallons of Wastewater
67 Pounds of Solid Waste

Left Coast Press made this paper choice because our printer, Thomson-Shore, Inc., is a member of Green Press Initiative, a nonprofit program dedicated to supporting authors, publishers, and suppliers in their efforts to reduce their use of fiber obtained from endangered forests.

For more information, visit www.greenpressinitiative.org

Environmental impact estimates were made using the Environmental Defense Paper Calculator. For more information visit: www.papercalculator.org.

Understanding American Icons

An Introduction to Semiotics

Illustrated by the Author

Arthur Asa Berger

Left Coast Press Inc.

Walnut Creek
California

LEFT COAST PRESS, INC.
1630 North Main Street, #400
Walnut Creek, CA 94596
http://www.LCoastPress.com

ISBN 978-1-61132-038-1 hardcover
ISBN 978-1-61132-039-8 paperback

Library of Congress Cataloging-in-Publication Data

Berger, Arthur Asa, 1933-
Understanding American icons : an introduction to semiotics / Arthur Asa Berger.
p. cm.
Includes bibliographical references.
ISBN 978-1-61132-038-1 (alk. paper) — ISBN 978-1-61132-039-8 (pbk. : alk. paper)
1. Semiotics—United States. I. Title.
P99.37.U5B47 2011
302.2—dc23

2011033962

Printed in the United States of America

∞™ The paper used in this publication meets the minimum requirements of American National Standard for Information Sciences—Permanence of Paper for Printed Library Materials, ANSI/NISO Z39.48–1992.

Contents

Preface

If our lives are dominated by a search for happiness, then perhaps few activities reveal as much about the dynamics of this quest—in all its ardour and paradoxes—than our travels. They express, however inarticulately, an understanding of what life might be about, outside of the constraints of work and of the struggle for survival. Yet rarely are they considered to present philosophical problems—that is, issues requiring thought beyond the practical. We are inundated with advice on where to travel to, but we hear little of why and how we should go, even though the art of travel seems naturally to sustain a number of questions neither so simple nor so trivial, and whose study might in modest ways contribute to an understanding of what the Greek philosophers beautifully termed eudaimonia, or "human flourishing."

Alain de Botton, *The Art of Travel*

Self-contempt and a sense of fraudulence distinguish the attitude of contemporary self-conscious travelers. There is a touching desperation in the attempts of professional tourists, well-funded anthropologists, and recording travelers, to distinguish themselves from the traveling masses and run-of-the-mill adventurers. The most characteristic mark of the tourist is the wish to avoid tourists and places they congregate. But this is merely evidence of the fact that travel is no longer a means of achieving distinction. It is a way or achieving and realizing a norm, the common identity we all share—the identity of the stranger.

Eric J. Leed, *The Mind of the Traveler: From Gilgamesh to Global Tourism*

When I started writing *American Icons: An Introduction to Semiotics,* I knew what methodologies I would be using in the book—semiotics allied with other disciplines and sciences in an approach generally known a cultural criticism—and I knew what I wanted to do: offer interpretations of a number of the most "iconic" buildings, structures and places in the United States. When we talk about something being "iconic," we mean it is culturally significant and its meaning is generally tied to history or some other quality that makes it important and memorable.

I soon found that I could devote much of the book to New York City, but I decided that a book on American icons should be more comprehensive, so I have not dealt with some iconic places and buildings in New York because I wanted to be able to deal with icons in other parts of the country. Thus, I have chapters on topics such as Fenway Park, the Mall of America, the Grand Canyon, the Space Needle, the Las Vegas strip, the Westin Bonaventure Hotel in Los Angeles, the Hoover Dam, the Alamo, Mt. Rushmore, and the Gold Country in California.

In each of my chapters I've tried to explain the cultural significance of the icon I was dealing with and to use theories and concepts that might help us see these icons in a more interesting light. In this book you will find that I have analyzed my icons by applying ideas from a number of theorists such as:

M.M.Bakhtin on carnivalization and feasting

Georg Simmel on the stranger

Sigmund Freud on anal eroticism, the unconscious and the id/ego/superego

Jean-François Lyotard on postmodernism and narratives

Ferdinand de Saussure on signs, concepts, and semiotic theory

C.S. Peirce on semiotic theory, icons, indexes and symbols

Jean Baudrillard on postmodernism, Disneyland, and consumer cultures

Erik Cohen on tourism and authenticity

Mircea Eliade on myth, sacred and profane space

Mark Gottdiener on socio-semiotics and Disneyland

Guy Debord on spectacle and capitalism

Henri Lefebvre on advertising and everyday life

Marshall McLuhan on advertising and the public mind

Hortense Powdermaker on Hollywood as a dream factory

Robert Venturi on what we can learn from Las Vegas

Frederick Jackson Turner on the frontier and American character and culture

Raymond Williams on Gramsci and hegemony

Dean MacCannell on the tourist as archetype

Fredrick Jameson on postmodernism and the Hotel Westin Bonaventure

Some of the icons I've dealt with, such as the Hoover Dam, the Cowboys Stadium, and the Gateway Arch in Saint Louis are examples of incredible feats of engineering. A number of the icons have historic significance, such as the Statue of Liberty, the San Francisco Chinatown, and the Alamo. Many chapters also tie the icons to racial, ethnic or cultural groups, such as African-Americans, American Indians, Chinese, Latinos, Iranians, Vietnamese and Jews.

In all cases, I have tried to tease out any cultural meanings attached to the icons and use whatever disciplines and theories I found relevant to help explain their importance. I have also used quotations from scholars and other sources as epigraphs before each analysis. These epigraphs offer us something to think about relative to the chapters in which they are found and are meant to enhance our understanding of the significance of each of the icons under consideration.

Alain de Botton points out that travel plays an important role in what we might describe as "the good life" and good living. Travel helps us recharge our batteries and provides many kinds of pleasures and gratifications. And Eric Leed explains that tourists are always, in a sense, strangers—even if they are visiting other parts of their own city, state, or country. I have approached the icons as a kind of stranger. As strangers we often see things that people who live in places we visit are not aware of; that is, we can be more objective and perceptive because the things we see are somewhat unfamiliar. I use "stranger" in the sense that the German sociologist George Simmel used the term. He wrote in a famous 1908 essay, "The Stranger," that strangers have the freedom to be objective. As he put it, "Objectivity may also be defined as freedom. The objective individual is bound by no commitments which could prejudice his perceptions, understanding and evaluation of the given" (in Levine 1971: 186).

The United States is a huge country and for the traveler it offers incredible diversity and any number of places to go and buildings to visit that are historically and culturally important. Some of them are even UNESCO World Heritage Sites, which means their importance is universally recognized. The British writer Matthew Arnold wrote about the importance of knowing "the best that had been thought and said." With this notion in mind, I have analyzed some of America's most important iconic tourist destinations, some of the best and most interesting places to see and visit. I would hope that my book will also help you understand their semiotic, psychological, social, cultural, political and historic importance and, perhaps, see them in a new light.

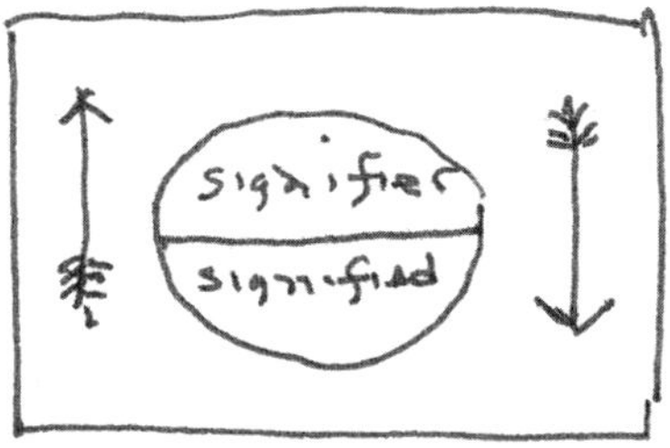

Chapter 1

Icons and Semiotics: An Introduction

It seems a strange thing, when one comes to ponder over it, that a sign should leave its interpreter to supply part of its meaning; but the explanation of the phenomenon lies in the fact that the entire universe—not merely the universe of existents, but all that wider universe, embracing the universe of existents, as a part, the universe which we are all accustomed to refer to as "the truth"—that all this universe is perfused with signs, if it not composed exclusively of signs.

C.S. Peirce, in T. Sebeok, *A Perfusion of Signs*

The basic unit of semiotics is the sign *defined conceptually as something that stands for something else, and, more technically, as a spoken or written word, a drawn figure, or a material object unified in the mind with a particular cultural concept. The sign is this unity of word-object, known as a* signifier *with a corresponding, culturally prescribed content or meaning, known as a* signified. *Thus our minds attach the word "dog," or the drawn figure of a "dog," as a signifier to the idea of a "dog," that is, a domesticated canine species possessing certain behavioral characteristics. If we came from a culture that did not possess dogs in daily life, however unlikely, we would not know what the signifier "dog" means.... When dealing with objects that are signifiers of certain concepts, cultural meanings, or ideologies of belief, we can consider them not only as "signs," but* sign vehicles. *Signifying objects carry meanings with them.*

Mark Gottdiener, *The Theming of America: Dreams, Visions and Commercial Spaces*

"This company is about icons."

That's how Patricio de Marco, the chief executive officer of Gucci, described the brand in an article about him in the *Wall Street Journal*. And most of the chief executives of upscale brands would say the same thing about their brands and their iconic logos. What they mean by describing their brands as iconic is that they are distinctive and known for being beautifully designed, well made and expensive. Gucci products can be identified by the Gucci logo—a mark that distinguishes Gucci products from other brands with which it competes.

The term "icon" is used by semioticians to stand for something that generates meaning by resemblance. Semiotics can be described as the science of signs—a sign being anything that can be used to stand for something else. A word is a sign; thus the word "tree" stands for a large leafy plant. Facial expressions are also signs. So are hairstyles, eyeglasses, clothes, body language, and just about everything else you can think of.

C.S. Peirce, one of the founding fathers of semiotics, believed that everything is a sign and once wrote that "the universe is perfused with signs, if not made up entirely of them." He explained that there are three kinds of signs: Icons, Indexes and Symbols:

> Every sign is determined by its object, either first, by partaking in the characters of the object, when I call a sign an *Icon*; secondly, by being really and in its individual existence connected with the individual object, when I call the sign an *Index*; thirdly, by more or less certainty that it will be interpreted as denoting the object, in consequence of a habit (which term I use as including a natural disposition), when I call the sign a *Symbol*. (In Sebeok 1976: 36)

We can see how these three kinds of signs work in the table below:

Icon	**Index**	**Symbol**
Resemblance	Relationships	Learned Meaning
Photograph	Smoke and Fire	Cross, Star of David, Crescent

Table 1.1 Peirce's Three Kinds of Signs

A sign, Peirce explained, represents something to someone. There is always someone interpreting what the sign means. Icons, for Peirce, communicate meaning by resembling something. Thus, a photograph resembles a person. Indexes communicate meaning by relationships, such as smoke that generally indicates fire. We have to learn the meaning of symbols. Many of the "icons" of fashion designers are really symbols (technically, a form of symbol called a logo), since the only way we can know what they stand for is by learning about them from advertising, generally speaking, and it is the symbolic meaning of many of the places and buildings I deal with that is what is most important.

The term "iconicity" has been modified in popular usage in recent years and now stands for some kind of exemplary and culturally significant place or thing. And in some cases, we use the term "icon" to refer to a person—a famous politician or performer of some kind. Technically, the word icon comes from the Greek *eikôn* which means image or likeness. In Greek and Russian Orthodox churches there are many beautiful painted icons of saints and other important religious figures.

When I was in high school, in the eleventh grade, one of my teachers called me an "iconoclast," which means, literally speaking, a breaker of icons and idols. In other words, my teacher meant that I was a nonconformist in my thinking. In a sense, much of my career as a scholar and writer has involved "breaking" idols—taking them apart or deconstructing their hidden meanings and considering their psychological, sociological, political and cultural impact. The approach that uses these disciplines is known as cultural studies—a kind of analysis that uses concepts from a variety of disciplines to understand the significance of whatever is being investigated.

In this book I will be interpreting the social and cultural significance of some of the most important iconic places, structures, and buildings in the United States, and, in many cases, using these icons for a discussion of topics related to their symbolic meaning. One of the more outstanding examples of analyzing icons is found in the French semiotician Roland Barthes's books *Mythologies* and *The Eiffel Tower and Other Mythologies*. In these books he deals with iconic aspects of French culture, such as "The New Citroen," "Plastic," "The Iconography of the Abbé Pierre" or "The Eiffel Tower" and offers a semiotically informed Marxist interpretation of them.

Barthes was influenced by the work of Ferdinand de Saussure, a Swiss linguist who was the other founding father of semiotics. He wrote in his book *Course in General Linguistics* (1915/1966:16):

> Language is a system of signs that express ideas, and is therefore comparable to a system of writing, the alphabet of deaf-mutes, symbolic rites, polite formulas, military signals, etc. But it is the most important of all these systems.
>
> *A science that studies the life of signs within society* is conceivable; it would be a part of social psychology and consequently of general psychology; I shall call it *semiology* (from Greek *sēmeîon* or "sign"). Semiology would show what constitutes signs, what laws govern them. Since the science does not yet exist, no one can say what it would be; but it has a right to existence, a place staked out in advance.

The term "semiotics" that Peirce used has replaced semiology in modern usage. From a semiotic perspective, the various icons that I'll be analyzing are all symbols or complex signs.

Saussure suggested that signs are made of two parts: a sound-object that he called a *signifier*, and a concept generated by the signifier called a *signified*. The relation that exists between a signifier and signified is culturally determined, not natural, which explains why the meaning of signs can change over time.

As Saussure wrote in his book *Course in General Linguistics* (1915/1966: 67):

> I propose to retain the word *sign [signe]* to designate the whole and to replace concept and sound-image respectively by *signified [signifié]* and *signifier [signifiant];* the last two terms have the advantage of indicating the opposition that separates them from each other and from the whole of which they are parts.

Saussure made another point that is important here. The meaning of concepts is relational; they don't have any meaning in themselves and the basic relationship among signs is opposition. As he explained (117–118):

> Concepts are purely differential and defined not by their positive content but negatively by their relations with the other terms of the system.

It is not "content" that determines meaning, but "relations" that exist in some kind of a system. The "most precise characteristic" of these concepts, he adds, "is in being what the others are not.... Signs function, then, not through their intrinsic value but through their relative position (118)."

He offered an insight into symbols that is worth considering. As he explained (68):

> One characteristic of the symbol is that it is never wholly arbitrary; it is not empty, for there is a rudiment of a natural bond between the signifier and the signified. The symbol of justice, a pair of scales, could not be replaced by just another symbol, such as a chariot.

Conventionally, the symbol of justice is a blind goddess holding a pair of scales. You can't use just anything that comes into your mind as a symbol of justice; there has to be some kind of connection.

An American writer, Maya Pines, offered a valuable way of thinking about semiotics. She wrote (1982:61):

> Everything we do sends messages about us in a variety of codes, semiologists contend. We are also on the receiving end of innumerable messages encoded in music, gestures, foods, rituals, books, movies, or advertisements. Yet we seldom realize that we have received such messages, and would have trouble explaining the rules under which they operate.

It is the task of semiotics to bring these rules to consciousness and to figure out how to decode the messages found in the topics she lists above and the topics of interest to us here—monuments and places that are deemed iconic and that have important symbolic significance.

There is one more matter of interest when it comes to a semiotic approach to iconic sights and that involves what Dean MacCannell calls "markers" in his book *The Tourist: A New Theory of the Leisure Class.* He describes "markers" as follows (1976:110):

> Usually, the first contact a sightseer has with a sight is not the sight itself but with some representation thereof.... Modifying everyday usage somewhat, I have adapted the term *marker* to mean information about a specific sight. The information by a sight marker often amounts to no more than the name of the sight, or its picture, or a plan or map of it.... My use of the term extends it to cover any information about a sight, including that found in travel books, museum guides, stories told by persons who have visited it, art history texts and lectures.

The point is, usually tourists come prepared with a good deal of prior information about iconic sights they visit; they seldom just stumble upon them, though that kind of thing is possible. These markers color our expectations of what we will find when we visit a sight and what kind of experience we can expect from our sight-seeing. These sights are what Gottdiener called, semiotically speaking, sign vehicles. They contain a good deal of information and have important cultural and historical relevance.

These insights about semiotics inform the analysis of American icons that I am to undertake. Since I will be dealing with icons, it is worth considering the most popular American tourism sites where these icons are located. According to a report in *Forbes* magazine (www.Forbes.com), for 2010 these sites were:

Tourist Site	**Number of Visitors**
1. Times Square, New York City	37.6 million
2. Las Vegas Strip, NV	**29.1 million**
3. National Mall and Memorial Parks Washington, D.C	25 million
4. Faneuil Hall Marketplace, Boston	19 million
5. Magic Kingdom, Walt Disney World, Orlando, FL.	17.1 million
6. Golden Gate National Recreation Area, San Francisco	**17 million**
7. Disneyland, Anaheim, CA	**14.7 million**
8. Fisherman's Wharf, San Francisco	10 million (tie)
9. Hollywood Walk of Fame, Los Angeles	**10 million (tie)**
10. Great Smoky Mountains National Park, NC/TN	9.5 million

Table 1.2 Most Popular Tourist Sites in the United States

I'm not sure how Forbes created its list, because it does not include the millions of visitors to the Mall of America and other popular sites. But it is useful as a reference point to begin my analysis. I have chapters on all the topics in boldface.

It's also useful to place tourism in the United States in a global perspective. What follows is a list of the most popular countries for international tourists for 2008 supplied by the United Nations World Tourist Organization (www.world-tourism.org):

Country	**International Visitors**
France	79.3 million
United States	58.0 million
Spain	57.3 million
China	57.3 million
Italy	42.7 million
United Kingdom	30.2 million
Ukraine	25.4 million
Turkey	25.6 million

Table 1.3 International Visitors Statistics

We can see from these two charts that, even taking into account that the data are from slightly different years, Times Square, with more than 37 million visitors, is a more popular tourist destination than the United Kingdom, Ukraine or Turkey. International tourism is a big business in the United States, and both international and American tourists tend to visit places of historical and cultural significance. In this book I will be analyzing and interpreting many of the more popular tourist sites that have iconic significance. Foreign tourists who come to America do so, in part, in search of iconic places that they know about, from reading or watching films, and wish to see with their own eyes. What I offer in this book is a kind of mosaic that analyzes some of our most important iconic sights and structures.

Chapter 2

Perspectives on American Society and Culture

Amongst the novel objects that attracted my attention during my stay in the United States, nothing struck me more forcibly than the general equality of condition among the people. I readily discovered the prodigious influence which this primary fact exercises on the whole course of society; it gives a particular direction to public opinion, and a peculiar tenor to the laws; it imparts new maxims to the governing authorities, and peculiar habits to the governed.

I soon perceived that the influence of this fact extends far beyond the political character and the laws of the country, and that it has no less empire over civil society than over the government; it creates opinions, gives birth to new sentiments, founds novel customs, and modifies whatever it does not produce.

Alexis de Tocqueville, *Democracy in America*

Americans by 1815 had formulated three major beliefs, each a complex of ideas. The first tenet assumed the dignity of human personality and asserted the conviction that that dignity could be realized only when the individual was free to express himself and to participate in decisions of vital importance to him. The second tenet assumed that principles of universal validity underlie the common life of men in society, the application of which to affairs makes possible the realization of freedom and dignity. The third tenet asserted that the nation created in 1776 exists as a corporate entity not only to further the peace and security of its citizens but to aid—at home and, by example, abroad—the cause of freedom and humane living.

Ralph Henry Gabriel, *The Course of American Democratic Thought*

Now that I've discussed icons and semiotic theory, let me say something about the second topic in my title: American culture and society. There have been countless books about American culture, character, society and politics by foreign travelers, sociologists, political scientists, anthropologists, pop culturists, media theorists, cultural studies theorists, and scholars in many other disciplines. DeTocqueville, a Frenchman who visited the United States in 1831, is generally considered to have written one of the most incisive interpretations of American culture and politics. He focused attention on our egalitarian institutions and coined the term "individualism," which I will discuss shortly, to describe an important aspect of the American national character.

Let me suggest that there isn't one America but a number of different Americas or American regions including New England, the East coast, the deep South, the Midwest, and the Pacific northwest and that there are considerable differences in Americans resulting from where they were born and grew up. This extends from dialects (I'm from Boston and don't pronounce my "r's") to food preferences (think of Southern Fried Chicken), religions (think of the Mormons in Utah) and political beliefs (the deep South in now very Republican and California now is very Democratic). Some writers have suggested that the only thing that unites Americans, in all our diversity, is fast food and the mass media.

Many writers and scholars have dealt with the importance of immigration in America and of the impact that immigrants have had upon American culture and society. There are some cities in California where children from sixty different countries who speak sixty different languages are attending school and are undergoing—to varying degrees—the process of Americanization that is part of going to public schools. Except for the Native Americans, everyone living in America is either an immigrant or a descendent of immigrants. America has been the focus of incredible mass migrations of people from Ireland, Germany, Eastern Europe, China, Africa, South America, Central America, Iran, Vietnam ... one could go on endlessly about the various countries who have sent hundreds of thousands, if not millions of people here. Americans trace their roots to almost every country and region in the world.

Scholars have used different metaphors to describe the immigrant experience in American society. Some have suggested we are a gigantic melting pot where immigrants tend to slough off their differences and blend in to American society. Think pea soup here. Others have used the beef stew analogy arguing that though we're in the same pot (America), we tend to maintain our differences—ethnic, religious, social and cultural—and so you get many distinctive kinds of hyphenated Americans such as Irish-Americans, African-Americans, Hispanic-Americans, Italian-Americans, Jewish-Americans and Iranian-Americans. For example, there are several hundred thousand Iranians who have settled near Los Angeles, forming an Iranian-American community. They have their own newspapers and media just like Eastern-European Jews who came to America many decades ago, settled in New York, and established their own newspapers, theaters, restaurants and various organizations to sustain Jewish life and maintain Jewish cultural identity. There is now a very large Hispanic population in the Southwestern states and many other states, and it is estimated that in a few decades, the Hispanic population in California will be the largest ethnic group in the state.

In this chapter I will discuss several analyses of American culture and society, starting with one of the most famous and insightful works, Alexis de Tocqueville's *Democracy in America.* The quotation at the beginning of this chapter, about the importance of equality in America, offers us an insight into an important aspect of American history: unlike most countries, we never had a hereditary aristocracy. DeTocqueville was impressed by the egalitarian nature of American society and used our egalitarianism to help explain American character, society and politics.

One of de Tocqueville's most insightful passages deals with the matter of individualism in America. He discusses the relationship that exists between egoism and individualism as follows (1956:192–193):

> I have shown how it is that, in ages of equality, every man seeks for his opinions within himself; I am now to show how it is that, in the same ages, all his feelings are turned towards himself alone. *Individualism* is a novel expression, to which a novel idea has given birth. Our fathers were only acquainted with *égoisme* (selfishness). Selfishness is a passionate and exaggerated love of self, which leads a man to connect everything with himself and to prefer himself to everything in the world. Individualism is a mature and calm feeling, which disposes each member of a community to sever himself from the mass of his fellows, and to draw apart with his family and his friends, so that after he has thus formed a little circle of his own, he willingly leaves society at large to itself.

The problem, he points out, is that individualism tends to destroy "the virtues of public life" and in the end turns into selfishness. What is more, individualism, DeTocqueville felt, tends to spread and assume the same importance as equality.

He contrasts egalitarian societies like America with aristocratic societies, where people remain in the same condition for many generations, where people have a sense of their past and an attachment to their forefathers and where people feel bound to one another, which leads to cooperation with others. Not so in America and egalitarian societies in which, DeTocqueville suggests, people become estranged from one another (194):

> As social conditions become more equal, the number of persons increases who, although they are neither rich nor powerful enough to exercise any great influence over their fellows, have nevertheless acquired or retained sufficient education and fortune to satisfy their own wants. They owe nothing to any man, they expect nothing from any man; they acquire the habit of always considering themselves as standing alone, and they are apt to imagine that their whole destiny is in their own hands.
>
> Thus, not only does democracy make every man forget his ancestors, but it hides his descendants and separates his contemporaries from him; it throws him back forever upon himself alone, and threatens in the end to confine him entirely within the solitude of his own heart.

Although *Democracy in America* was first published more than 150 years ago, DeTocqueville's analysis of American culture, character and society still rings true, and helps explain the sense of alienation and powerlessness that many people feel in contemporary American society.

The other quotation in the epigraph, from a classic study of American democratic thought by Ralph Henry Gabriel, suggests that there have been three themes that have dominated American thought:

the belief in the importance of individual freedom,

the belief in a universal "fundamental moral law," and

the belief in an American mission—to spread democracy and freedom everywhere.

Gabriel's book was written in 1956, but his insights are still relevant. Thus, for example, on March 19, 2011, President Obama gave a speech in which he asserted that the president of Libya had violated the rights of all human beings—that is, fundamental moral law. Implicit in Obama's talk were the notions that individual freedom is important and that America, and other countries, has a duty or mission—to spread democracy.

There have been any number of other analyses of American culture and society that stress such matters as:

The importance of the frontier and nature in American thought

The impact of the American Revolution

The role of immigration

The development of nationalism

The significance of Feminism and the role of women

The role of Puritanism and religion in general

The importance of abundance

The development of a powerful consumer culture

The impact of postmodernism on American culture

The American as an Adamic or Adam-like (innocent) heroic figure

The American Dream

The importance of pragmatism

The impact of slavery and the growth of a "north-south" divide in the United States

The development of cities

The role of popular culture and the mass media

The importance of Europe as a "fatherland"

The question of American exceptionalism

The lack of a hereditary aristocracy

You will find discussions of these topics appearing in various places in this book. Thus, for example, my analyses of Disneyland and of the Mall of America deal with American popular culture and our consumer culture, as do my discussions of Graceland and the Las Vegas Strip. My analysis of the Grand Canyon draws upon the impact of the frontier and our attitudes toward nature and our sense of America as a kind of Adamic paradise full of people who have escaped the corruption of our European fatherland. I offer Mt. Rushmore as a good example of how nationalism has shaped our creation of monuments. The St. Louis Gateway Arch and Santa Fe can be connected to the development of cities and nationalism.

Many of the attempts to understand America have looked for a key concept to explain things, such as DeTocqueville's notion that our belief in equality is the basis of everything else that developed here or the idea that American society and politics reflect a continuing conflict between our core values of equality and individualism (as reflected in individual achievement).

This theme was developed in political sociologist Seymour Martin Lipset's *The First New Nation: The United States in Historical and Comparative Perspective.* Lipset begins his book as follows, sketching out two conflicting perspectives about what American society is like (1963:1):

> There has been a quite extraordinary number of books published in recent years that seek to analyze American society. Among the most widely read and talked about have been the works of Vance Packard, especially *The Status Seekers; The Power Elite* by C. Wright Mills; *The Organization Man* by William H. Whyte; *The Lonely Crowd* by David Riesman.... These and other works arrive at roughly two sorts of conclusions.
>
> According to the first view, America suffers from elaborate corruption in business and labor, and in law enforcement practices; from a growing concentration of business power; from the influences of mass media run by entertainment tycoons who satisfy the lowest common denominator in popular taste; and from a wasteful expenditure of resources directed to the enhancement of social status. According to the other view, American is an affluent, highly democratic society in which the distribution of income, of status symbols, and of opportunities for social mobility is becoming more even-handed all the time; in which tolerance for differences in culture, religion, and race is growing; and in which demand for the best in art, literature, and music is increasing.

Lipset's book was published in 1963 and since then, I would argue, the first view of American society has turned out to be more accurate than the second one. Statistics about income distribution, for example, show that the top one percent of Americans have more wealth than the bottom ninety percent. Nevertheless, there are people who believe that the matters discussed in the second view are more correct, and they have some evidence to support their view.

What is of interest to us here, relative to DeTocqueville's discussion of American character, involves Lipset's analysis of the tension that exists between two core values in America: equality and achievement.

As he explains (101):

> Two themes, equality and achievement, emerged from the interplay between the Puritan tradition and the Revolutionary ethos in the early formation of America's institutions. In this section, the thesis is advanced that the dynamic interaction of these two predominant values has been a constant element in determining American institutions and behavior. As we have seen, equalitarianism was an explicit part of the revolt against the traditions of the Old World, while an emphasis upon success and hard work had long been part of the Protestant ethic.

Like de Tocqueville before him, Lipset argued that certain key features of American character and life played a major role in shaping our society, politics and culture. From these basic concepts, Lipset could discuss any number of aspects of American politics and society.

We do not have a long national history and did not have a traditional aristocracy that helped generate a sense of the past and confirm a national identity. We also come from many different countries. This has led to a kind of obsession here with making sense of American culture and society. On July 21, 2011, I checked Google for sites dealing with America and Amazon.com for books on these topics. This is what I found:

Topic	**Google Sites**	**Amazon.com Books**
American culture	66,400,000	29,124
American society	106,000,000	123,000
American character	29,500,000	14,622
American civilization	5, 310,000	6,971

We can see that these topics are of enormous interest and that there are thousands of books on American character, society and culture.

Not having a hereditary aristocracy and not being a society based on class differences has led to all kinds of curious things in America. Our egalitarian and individualist culture has shaped the design of cities such as Los Angeles (with mile upon mile of small bungalows and little public transportation); the architecture of Las Vegas, with its hyper-phallic signs; and the creation of gigantic sports stadiums, such as the incredible Cowboys Stadium in Texas. Our new technological gizmos, such as iPads and iPhones, and new Internet sites such as Facebook that play such an important part in our lives can be seen as a triumph of American pragmatism and technological prowess, but also a reflection of the fact that many Americans feel isolated and lonely—the price we pay for our individualism.

Statistics show that the average American spends more than eight hours a day staring at screens: television screens, computer monitors, cell phone screens, tablet screens, and so on. We spend a great deal of time with these gizmos connecting with other people, to conduct business but also to help us deal with our loneliness. After a relatively brief fling with European modernism architecture, we rejected it in favor of postmodern architecture as reflected in the Las Vegas Strip, Disneyland, the Hotel Westin Bonaventure in Los Angeles, and many other important buildings in Los Angeles, New York, Portland, Oregon, and elsewhere.

We might say that our egalitarianism has led to a certain amount of excess in American culture, for there can be no end to our attempts to demonstrate, often by conspicuous consumption, that we are successful, and there is a certain insecurity we feel about ourselves and our lives and our prospects that I find pervasive in America.

To this point I have dealt with semiotic theory, which explains how we find meaning in words and images and other aspects of life, and with attempts to understand American character and culture by travelers and social scientists. Now I will begin with my analysis of American icons, and I start with one of our most important and popular ones—Disneyland.

Chapter 3

Disneyland

In the fall of 1928, an eager young actor was introduced at a New York movie house to rave reviews. He wasn't very handsome, with protruding ears like Bing Crosby, and a wider mouth than Martha Ray. His voice was high-pitched, yes squeaky. But, of even more significance, he was not even human, but belonged to the rodent family.

Michael Brody, M.D., "The Wonderful World of Disney—Its Psychological Appeal"

Disneyland is a perfect model of all the entangled orders of simulacra. It is first of all a play of illusions and phantasms: the Pirates, the Frontier, the Future World, etc. This imaginary world is supposed to ensure the success of the operation. But what attracts the crowds most is without doubt the social microcosm, the religious, *miniaturized pleasure of real America, of its constraints and joys. One parks outside and stands in line inside, one is altogether abandoned at the exit. The only phantasmagoria in this imaginary world lies in the tenderness and warmth of the crowd, and in the sufficient and excessive number of gadgets necessary to create the multitudinous effect. The contrast with the absolute solitude of the parking lot—a veritable concentration camp—is total.*

Jean Baudrillard, *The Precession of Simulacra*

Disney describes how he created Mickey Mouse. He is quoted in Richard Schickel's *The Disney Version* (1968, 95):

> His head was a circle with an oblong circle for a snout. The ears were also circles so they could be drawn the same no matter how he turned his head.
>
> His body was like a pear and he had a long tail. His legs were pipestems and we stuck them in big shoes [also circular] to give him the look of a kid wearing his father's shoes.
>
> We didn't want him to have mouse hands, because he was supposed to be more human. So we gave him gloves. Five fingers looked like too much on such a little figure, so we took one away. That was just one less finger to animate.
>
> To provide a little detail, we gave him the two-button pants. There was no mouse hair or any other frills that would slow down animation.

We can see in this statement Disney's desire to subordinate the creative process to the demands of technology. It was the need to be able to crank out Mickey Mouse images quickly that determined the way he looks. Disney was obliged to produce 700 feet of film every two weeks and needed a figure that was easy to draw.

This attention to detail and control was to animate his films and later his theme parks. He offered the following comments on the opening of Disneyland on July 17, 1955 (www.disneydream.com/DLOopen.htm):

> To all who come to this happy place, welcome. Disneyland is your land. Here age relives fond memories of the past...and here youth may savor the challenge and promise of the future. Disneyland is dedicated to the ideals, the dreams, and the hard facts that have created America...with the hope that it will be a source of joy and inspiration to all the world.

Disney had taken his children to amusement parts and was disturbed by how dirty and tawdry they were. His innovation was to create a theme park, based on his film characters, that was clean and wholesome. We can find the impact of Puritanism and our reverence for nature in Disney's feelings about amusement parks.

Jan Morris, one of the best travel writers of our times, found herself feeling "uneasy" in Disneyland. As she explains in an article on "Los Angeles: The Know-How City" in *Rolling Stone* in 1976 and republished in a collection of her essays, *Destinations: Essays from Rolling Stone* (1982:98):

> For myself, I am left with an uneasy feeling, even about Disneyland, where the most advanced technical resources, the most brilliant

> administrative systems, are used simply to animate a gigantic charade. The sham treads uncomfortably upon the heels of truth, and one begins to wonder whether a dummy castle from Snow White, a make-believe New Orleans restaurant, even a nonalcoholic mint julep might not be as good, and as true, as the real thing. I found this inescapable illusion rather suffocating, and was revived, as I staggered from the King Arthur Carousel to the Casey Jr. Circus Train, through Tomorrowland to the Bear Country, only by the presence of the peripatetic bands, blues, brass, or Mexican, who really were undeniably alive and irreplaceable by electronics even in L.A.

Morris is a great travel writer because her perceptions and her feelings about the places she visits are so interesting and her use of the English language is so superb. The adjectives with which she describes Disneyland, "uneasy" and "suffocating," offer us an insight into the ambience of Disneyland that is at odds with the way it describes itself and the way it wants people to think about it.

Disneyland advertises itself as "the happiest place on earth," but is it? In an article by a psychiatrist, Michael Brody, "The Wonderful World of Disney," we get a different picture. In the first part of his essay he deals with anal themes in Disney's cartoons and other work and quotes Richard Schickel who described Disney in *The Disney Version* as follows, "There was always something obsessive about Walt Disney's personality. There was his parsimony, his single-minded concentration, and his need for order and details" (1976: 350). This description of Disney's personality is very similar to Sigmund Freud's description of anal erotics (in *Freud: Character and Culture*, edited by Philip Rieff (1963: 27–28):

> The persons I am about to describe are remarkable for a regular combination of the three following peculiarities: they are exceptionally *orderly, parsimonious,* and *obstinate.*
>
> Each of these words really covers a small group of series of traits which are related to one another. "Orderly" comprises both body cleanliness and reliability and conscientiousness in the performance of petty duties: the opposite of it would be untidy and negligent. "Parsimony" may be exaggerated up to the point of avarice; and obstinacy may amount to defiance, with which irascibility and vindictiveness may easily be associated.

There are good reasons, then, to suggest that Walt Disney had elements of anal eroticism in his personality and that his psychological makeup was to be reflected in his films and in Disneyland, the only theme park that he personally created.

Brody then discusses Disneyland from a psychoanalytic perspective and writes (March, 1976: 350):

> Here, in "his" magic kingdom he would come after nightfall to pick up litter missed by his army of sanitation workers. Disney strove for control over his work and destiny. What could be more natural that a huge, controlled playground, where all could be Disney-regulated.
>
> There is excellent crowd control here. We are led on by the next attraction up the street. Lines may be long, but broken up into smaller units, they appear shorter.
>
> Employees are young and clean-cut. All go to a training school for smile and behavior regulation.
>
> Most of the attractions are computerized, with their stars an agent's dream, well-controlled examples of yet another Disney marvel: audio-animatronics.... The overall park environment couldn't be cleaner, or neater in Florida, even the lakes, forests and beaches are ecologically planned. Waste baskets blend with the scenery and there is even a crew of chewing gum scrapers. "Dirty" money is exchanged for clean, fresh colorful coupons.

As a result of all this regulation and compartmentalization, Brody explains, you also find passivity. People who attend the park have little to do except become receptacles of experiences. "Except for a penny arcade," he writes, "there are no skills to be tested or games to be played" (358).

The folksy "Uncle Walter" exterior, the genial and amiable "Walt," was a mask for a person driven by powerful unconscious forces that helped shape his great creation, Disneyland, where everyone could be subtly controlled and their behavior regulated. Naming the park after himself also suggests an element of narcissism and maybe even grandiosity. One question we may ask is this—does the popularity of Disneyland, with its anal themes, reflect the same psychological attributes of the people who go there or is Disneyland a kind of momentary vacation from freedom to enjoy the pleasures of structure and control.

Many scholars have found interesting things to say about Disneyland, Disneyworld and the whole Disney phenomenon. Socio-semiotician Mark Gottdiener offers some important insights in a paper, "Disneyland: A Utopian Urban Space," that appeared in the *Journal of Contemporary*

Ethnography. He discusses a topic Brody mentioned, the matter of social control, and writes (1982: 139):

> In Disneyland social control is refined to an art, the art of moving crowds by their own motivation instead of coercion. D-land represents the ideal in this regard. It is the perfection of subordination: people digging their own fantasy graves. Los Angeles, in contrast, is the site of the coercive mechanisms of wage labor, ideology, and state power. This space also controls by the separation and isolation of people.

He compares the kind of subtle social control found in Disneyland with Los Angeles, where real-world considerations are the mechanisms of social control.

Then he moves on to another topic, namely the "illusion" people attending Disneyland have about its costs and the way the cost of entering Disneyland acts as a filter mechanism screening out poor people who can't afford its admission fees. Disneyland thus becomes a utopian classless, all middle-class, micro-society.

> Disneyland presents the illusion of cornucopia. After paying a lump sum at the entrance to the park, participants enjoy an abundance of opportunity for amusement. Prior to the 1980s rides were portioned out by varied individual prices, some of which were relatively expensive. Since July 1981 the lump sum payment, which is over $20 a person, now allows visitors to unlimited access to all rides—a true cornucopia, if you can afford the entrance fee.
>
> In the theme park space, class distinctions are minimized and ignored, because the poor have been screened out of the park by the price of admission. In this world, corporate control is benevolent and even paternal. A ride is "brought to you by," "with the compliments of," and "presented by." These epithets are unobtrusive and subliminal. They are extended in the manner of a gift, therefore they invoke the traditional economy of a tribal society. The insidious implication here is that such courtesies are reciprocal. (140)

Gottdiener turns his attention, next, to two interesting matters: first, he suggests that Disneyland can be considered a postmodern kind of entertainment that simulates the past and idealizes what might be described as a mythic "small town" America. I deal with postmodernism in more detail in my discussion of the Bonaventure Hotel in Los Angeles. Briefly, postmodernism involves a loss of faith in the wide ranging philosophies and belief systems that have guided us over the years. Postmodern societies are media-saturated consumer cultures that do not recognize major differences between elite culture and popular culture, among other things.

In addition, in Disneyland, there is role reversal and children make the most important decisions. As Gottdiener explains (140):

> In Disneyland, the built environment is entertaining. Every edifice has symbolic value, much as was the case for ancient and medieval cities. Disneyland, as the most successful theme park, helped inaugurate the entertainment culture of postmodernism.
>
> Finally, Disneyland inverts the structure of family authority. While most families, regardless of class, are adult-directed even if they are child-centered, a visit to D-land is ostensibly for children (or tourist visitors who then are ascribed the status of children). Here the child gets to direct the adults. Invariably they choose the rides, the food, and the schedule. Parents become chaperones or vicarious thrill seekers through the eyes of their own offspring.

This role that parents take in Disneyland seems to have spread beyond the confines of Disney's creations and now, increasingly, young children are involved in decisions parents make about purchasing cars and other things.

Gottdiener offers a semiotically informed analysis of Disney's creations and Disney's important role in American culture, but he doesn't adequately explain why so many children and adults love going to Disneyland and why Disneylands in many foreign countries have become important destinations for travelers and tourists. The source of Disneyland's international appeal remains something of an enigma.

Sharon Zukin, in her book *Point of Purchase: How Shopping Changed American Culture,* suggests that Disneyland became the model for stores and thus has played an important role in our consumer culture. She writes (2005:221):

> Disneyland has shaped much of our thinking about the social spaces of stores. As a merchandising model, Disneyland suggests the advantages a store can draw from providing "circuses"—attractions besides the merchandise—in order to give shoppers a "memorable experience."

Disney has, in fact, created its own stores that sell its products, tying itself into its role as an archetype of American popular culture and trying, as Zukin puts it, to spread the Disney "aura" everywhere. This connection of theme parks and shopping malls is one that I will discuss in my analysis of the Mall of America.

Disney's ubiquitous impact and its cultural resonance may explain why the French sociologist Jean Baudrillard took so much interest in Disney. He suggested, in an audacious reversal of things, that Disneyland is the reality and the United States should be seen as a simulation of Disneyland. As Baudrillard explained in an article "Disney World Company" (*Liberation,* translated by Francois Debrix):

> Disney, the precursor, the grand initiator of the imaginary as virtual reality, is now in the process of capturing all the real world to integrate it into a synthetic universe, in the form of a vast "reality show," where reality itself becomes a spectacle, where the real becomes a theme park. (www.egs/edu/faculty/jean-baudrillard/articles/disneyworld-company/, March 4, 1996)

In his celebrated article "The Precession of Simulacra," Baudrillard (1995) expanded his analysis of Disneyland:

> Everywhere in Disneyland the objective profile of America, down to the morphology of individuals and of the crowd, is drawn. All its values are exalted by the miniature and the comic strip.... Disneyland exists in order to hide that it is the "real" country, all of "real" America that *is* Disneyland.... Disneyland is presented as imaginary in order to make us believe that the rest is real, whereas all of Los Angeles and the America that surrounds it are no longer real, but belong to the hyperreal order and to the order of simulation. (www.egs/ed/faculty/jean-baudrillard/articles/simulacra-and-simulations-i-the-precession-of-simulacra/, February 15, 1995)

For Baudrillard, Disneyland shows the power of Disney's iconic creations—the fake castles, the mock small town America, and so on, to shape our consciousness and, in the form of simulacra, that is "simulations" or imitations of reality, provide people with a fantastic and erratic perception of reality.

Disney himself was cryogenized—frozen immediately after he died by a company that keeps dead people in that state until hoped-for new developments allow them to be unfrozen and returned to life. Maybe, at some future date, if technology evolves the way Disney hoped it will, he will rise from the dead, and when he thaws out, God only knows what else he will think of to further "entertain" Americans and "capture" those elements of humanity that fall into his hands by visiting his parks.

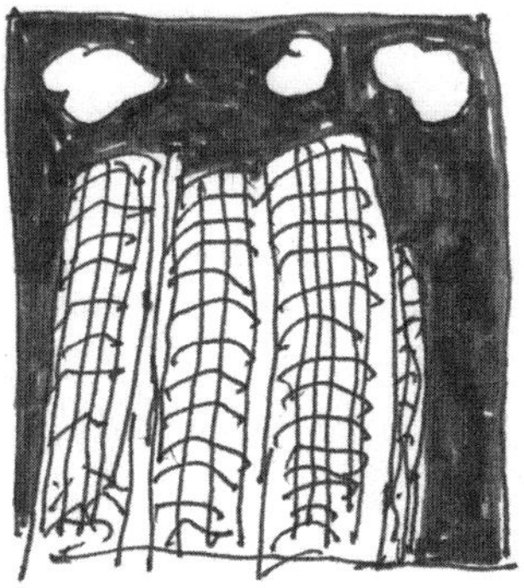

Chapter 4

The Westin Bonaventure Hotel in Los Angeles

Given the absolute symmetry of the four towers, it is quite impossible to get your bearings in this lobby; recently, color coding and directional signals have been added in a pitiful and revealing, rather desperate, attempt to restore the coordination of an older space. I will take as the most dramatic practical result of this spatial mutation the notorious dilemma of the shop-keepers on the various balconies: it has been obvious since the opening of the hotel in 1977 that nobody could ever find any of these stores, and unlikely to be as fortunate a second time; as a consequence, the commercial tenants are in despair and all the merchandise is marked down to bargain prices....

So I come to my principal point here, that this latest mutation in space—postmodern hyperspace—has finally succeeded in transcending the capacities of the individual human body to locate itself, to organize its immediate surroundings perceptually, and cognitively to map its position in a mappable external world. It may now be suggested that this alarming disjunction point between the body and its built environment—which is to the initial bewilderment of the older modernism as the velocities of spacecraft to those of the automobile—and itself stand as the symbol and analogon of that ever sharper dilemma which is the incapacity of our minds, at least at present, to map the great global multinational and decentered communicational network in which we find ourselves caught as individual subjects.

Fredric Jameson, *Postmodernism or, The Cultural Logic of Late Capitalism*

The Westin Bonaventure Hotel at the edge of downtown Los Angeles is one of the more iconic hotels in the United States. It was designed by a celebrated architect, John C. Portman, Jr., and has played an important role in American popular culture, appearing in films such as *This is Spinal Tap, Escape from LA, Buck Rogers in the 25th Century* and the video game *Grand Theft Auto*. It is 35 stories tall, has 1,354 rooms and 135 suites, and is the largest hotel in Los Angeles.

The most expensive suites cost more than $2,000 a night. The hotel consists of four mirror-skinned, glistening, thirty-five story towers (with a fifth core tower inside) and has been described by Frederic Jameson, in a very controversial analysis, part of which was cited above, as an important postmodern structure, though it also contains modernist elements.

It is the disorientation that people experience in the Bonaventure's lobby and the amusement park qualities and shifting perspectives people feel while walking in the lobby that are important postmodern features of the hotel. Literally speaking, the term postmodern means "coming after" modernism. The term "post" means "after" but it can also mean "moving beyond," "different from," or "the opposite of." What we call the modernist period, culture theorists suggest, dominated our cultural life between 1900 and 1960. The postmodernist period, then, involves the years from 1960 to the present. Postmodernist thinkers believe that in advanced societies there was a sudden "cultural mutation" around 1960, and that this mutation, this remarkable change in beliefs, attitudes, philosophies and aesthetic sensibilities, is what is explained by postmodernism. It replaced modernism in our arts, literature and other aspects of culture.

A French scholar, Jean-François Lyotard, discusses postmodernism in terms of narratives in his book *The Postmodern Condition: A Report on Knowledge* (1984: *xxiv*):

> Simplifying to the extreme, I define *postmodern* as incredulity toward metanarratives. This incredulity is undoubtedly a product of progress in the sciences: but that progress in turn presupposes it. To the obsolescence of the metanarrative apparatus of legitimation corresponds, most notably, the crisis of metaphysical philosophy and of the university institution which in the past relied on it. The narrative function is losing its functors, its great hero, its great dangers, its great voyages, its great goal.

This statement, in which Lyotard defines postmodernism as involving "incredulity toward metanarratives," is probably the most famous definition of the term ever written. We no longer have faith, Lyotard argues, in modernism's all-encompassing, wide-ranging meta-narratives—the systems of thought (as expounded in religions, political ideologies and philosophy) that have grounded us in the past. Instead, in a postmodern world, we have many different narratives vying for our attention, which has led to a crisis of legitimation. Who has the answers to our questions? Whose beliefs are valid? What's right and wrong? Can we privilege one point of view about anything over another?

To understand postmodernism it is useful to contrast it with the modernism that preceded it. The term "modern" comes from the fifth-century Latin word *modernus,* which was used to differentiate the pagan era from the Christian era. As Lyotard understands the term, modernism is based on acceptance of grand narratives. I spell out the implications of this belief system in a chart that follows.

Modernism	**Postmodernism**
1900 to 1960	1960 to present
The Biltmore Hotel	The Westin Bonaventure Hotel
Metanarratives	Incredulity toward metanarratives
Unified, coherent self	Fragmented, shattered, decentered self
Differentiation	De-differentiation
Seriousness	Playfulness, ironic stances
Print culture	Electronic culture
Books	Cell phones, tablets, Kindles
New York architecture	Las Vegas architecture
Mies Van der Rohe	Philip Johnson (AT&T skyscraper)
Unitary works of art	The pastiche (pieces patched together)
Production society (make)	Consumer cultures (buy)
Reality	Hyperreality
America	Disneyland

Table 4.1 Modernism and Postmodernism Contrasted

Postmodernism develops at the same time that consumer capitalism becomes dominant and thus postmodernism is associated with consumer culture and mass consumption which affect fashion and shape peoples' lifestyles. We live now, postmodernist theorists suggest, in a world dominated by media, images, and simulations of reality; this world of signs has undermined our sense of reality and dissolved our sense that there are fixed structures and stable boundaries, that anything has meaning. Like so many belief systems, postmodernism is intimately connected to the system it rejected and replaced—modernism.

I will now discuss some of the differences between postmodernism and modernism that were mentioned in my chart. First, if modernism involves differentiation (between the elite arts and popular culture), postmodernism involves what can be described as de-differentiation, breaking down the barriers between the elite arts and popular culture and reveling joyfully in mass culture. If modernism involves a "high seriousness" towards life, postmodernism involves an element of game playing and an ironic stance. In postmodernist societies, people "play" with their identities, changing them when they feel bored with their old ones.

If modernism involves stylistic purity, as reflected visually in modernist architecture, postmodernism involves stylistic eclecticism and variety, with the pastiche as the governing metaphor. If modernism believes we can know reality, postmodernism argues that we are all confounded by illusions and what the French sociologist Jean Baudrillard called "hyperreality," as exemplified in Disneyland. Postmodernism is the realm of consumer culture, in contrast to what we might call the production culture of modernism. The heroes of modernism are the great businessmen and statesmen while the heroes of postmodernism tend to be celebrities and entertainment figures, whose tastes and consumption habits are held up as models to us all.

If postmodern theory were just an interesting notion that philosophers debated about, but which had little or no impact on our everyday lives, it probably wouldn't have achieved the notoriety it has gained. The argument of postmodernist theorists is that postmodernism has profoundly affected our societies and the way we live, whether or not we are aware of this being the case. People may not be aware that their thinking and behavior have been affected by postmodernism, just as schizophrenics are not aware that they are suffering from that mental illness.

4. *The Westin Bonaventure Hotel in Los Angeles*

In a chapter on "Postmodernism and Architecture" in the *Routledge Companion to Postmodernism,* architectural critic Diane Morgan discusses the "placelessness" of the Bonaventure Hotel (2005: 77):

> Another theorist who... takes a stand against the prevailing placelessness of postmodern architecture, is Fredric Jameson.... For Jameson, the summation of postmodern despair, the total abandonment of any attempt to contribute positively to the urban environment, is encapsulated by the Bonaventura Hotel in Los Angeles. This building frustrates the experience of place.... It discourages independent mobility, obliging the unsuspecting visitors passively to give themselves up to its "transportation machines" which conduct them from one isolated point to another.

Morgan agrees with Jameson that the Bonaventure Hotel is what we might describe as an anti-human monstrosity.

Jack Solomon, a semiotician at the University of California in Los Angeles, is another culture critic who finds the Bonaventure Hotel fascinating. In his book, *The Signs of Our Times: The Secret Meaning of Everyday Life,* he compares the Bonaventure Hotel with a hotel that is near it, the Biltmore Hotel, built in 1923. It was built, he writes, while the Los Angeles downtown was thriving and thus placed itself facing Pershing Square with an element of assurance. The Bonaventure Hotel is a few blocks from Pershing Square in an area that was rundown but has been renewed in recent years. Solomon suggests that the design of the Bonaventure Hotel isolates it from its environment.

He describes the Bonaventure as follows (1996:116):

> The Bonaventure thrusts five mirrored-glass cylinders into the L.A. sky. But though the views of the city from the top are breathtaking, there are no such views from the bottom. As you sit by one of the three pools on the ground floor, or in one of the many concrete "pods" that hang above them, you see nothing of the street. Glass skylighting illuminates indoor "sidewalk cafes" that seem to belong to an idealized Parisian boulevard, while the careful concealment of the Bonaventure's entrances and exits completes the illusion of a utopian public park with clear vertical views to the sky but no horizontal views to the less than utopian conditions outside.

The Biltmore, Solomon suggests, can be seen as a "relic of aristocratic self-assurance and power," in contrast to the Bonaventure which generates a vision of a utopian future except that, for critics of postmodernism, it is an anti-utopian and anti-human vision that the Bonaventure projects. This can be seen in the feelings we get when we are in the lobby and become confused and disoriented.

Solomon adds that while the Bonaventure, which is "all democratic steel and glass and concrete" seems, at first glance, like a modernist building, it isn't modernist at all. The four glass towers are arranged around a fifth cylinder at the core of the structure and the design of the building seems abstract enough to qualify as a modernist building, but when one is in the hotel, its postmodernist characteristics become quite apparent.

Jameson based much of his critique of the Bonaventure on the sense of disorientation people feel on the ground floor of the hotel, and Solomon's description of the ground floor is similar in nature. He writes (1990:119):

> Consider the view from the ground floor. In actuality, the floor plan of the Bonaventure constitutes a rectangular space centered on a cylindrical core, but the effect at ground level is that of a decentered circle. As you stroll from poolside café to poolside café round the perimeter of this confusing space, the central core is alternatively concealed and revealed by the intricately planned landscaping, promoting the illusion of a shifting center by constantly varying your visual perspective. You feel that you are walking in a circle, but it is a circle that has been inscribed within a square. This is not only disorienting; it also has something of the symbolic effect of King Arthur's Round Table because here no space can claim priority of place over another.

The decentered circle that Solomon talks about suggests the kind of decentered lives, pervaded by illusions and mass mediated pop culture, that we lead in postmodern societies.

Solomon adds that the lobby of the Bonaventure, with its twelve elevators and eleven escalators, reminds him, in some ways, of an amusement park. He also suggests that buildings like the Bonaventure may be affecting the design of upscale contemporary homes that feature "towering atrium ceilings" and "grandiose" living rooms. Let me suggest that it is the postmodern aspects of the Bonaventure that have affected home design just as postmodernism affects our everyday lives in profound ways. This can be seen very directly in our architecture.

In his book, *After the Great Divide: Modernism, Mass Culture, Postmodernism,* Andreas Huyssen writes that it is in architecture that we see, most clearly, how postmodernism has broken away from modernism. He offers the example of the great modernist Dutch architect Mies van der Rohe, whose "glass curtain walls"—that is, huge slabs of windows—differ profoundly from the work of postmodern architects, with their use of mixed styles. Thus, he cites, as a typical postmodern building, Philip Johnson's famous AT&T skyscraper in New York City which has a Roman colonnade at its street level, a neoclassical midsection, and a Chippendale pediment at its top.

Architecture, like all the arts, feeds on certain sensibilities that are found in a given time period. In this case, the Johnson building is a repudiation of modernist architecture, with its monotonous slabs of windows and an extreme simplification of style. Las Vegas, as I discuss in my chapter on the city, is a place where the eclecticism shown in the Johnson building is found permeating the whole strip. The same sensibility found in the Johnson building and in the Bonaventure Hotel, the same desire for newness and eclecticism, affects music, painting, drama, film, many other arts and, ultimately, the way we live our lives, as well. And that is because these arts, I would suggest, whether we recognize it or not, have an impact on our individual psyches and affect the way we think about things and the way we live.

Chapter 5

The St. Louis Gateway Arch

Like a silver rainbow glistening upon the Midwestern horizon, The Gateway Arch has always suggested a promise of new opportunities within the constantly shifting order of modern American society. The 630 foot stainless steel Gateway Arch is the symbolic centerpiece of the St. Louis riverfront, a man-made natural park carved out of the city's historic riverfront in honor of Thomas Jefferson and America's frontier experience.... The project marked time during the 1950s, while the space-age technology employed during its construction in the early 1960s made it a perfect symbol of the New Frontier ethos of that period. In the 1970s and 1980s it became a catalyst for downtown redevelopment, a major national tourist attraction, a fairground for a major media event, and an advertising logo.

W. Arthur Mehroff, *The Gateway Arch: Fact & Symbol*

The most important symbol that identifies St. Louis to the rest of the nation, and for that matter the world, is the monumental Gateway Arch. This enormous structure towers over the St. Louis waterfront and is visited by millions each year. Plans for the Arch began as early as the 1930s, when city officials began to demolish the area in preparation for the grounds for the Jefferson National Memorial Park. Several years later in 1948, famed Finnish sculptor Eero Saarinen won the design competition. Work was not completed until the 1960s. The famed Arch looms in the city's skyscape. Built of shiny stainless steel, it seems to reach towards heaven like the cathedrals of old.

Al Montesi and Richard Deposki, *Downtown St. Louis*

In Mehroff's book (1992), he describes how the Gateway Arch led to a major transformation in the way inhabitants of the city thought about themselves and their city. Eventually, and perhaps inevitably, the Arch also became highly commercialized and was used "to sell appliances, automobiles, newspapers, television programs, even the city of St. Louis itself" (5).

What we find with the Gateway Arch is an example of what we might call "The Frank Gehry Phenomenon," in which a "world-class" building (in this case Gehry's famous museum in Bilbao) puts a city on the map—or, more precisely, on the tourist map as a "must-see" city. The building leads, then, to the economic and physical development of the city as a tourist destination, which is what happened in St. Louis. The Gateway Arch also provides a certain kind of psychic boost to the inhabitants of the city who see themselves, now, as living in a place with a significant iconic structure.

Symbols, we must realize, have considerable power and resonance. In his book *Symbols and Civilization,* Ralph Ross discusses the way symbols work (1962:167):

> Symbols…may be words, things, or actions. They are conventional signs which can be interpreted properly only by knowing their socially determined meanings.… They develop out of the needs and uses of each society. They reflect the experiences of the people by the objects and relations they symbolize, and the values of the culture by the emphases they provide. Symbols often have meanings in addition to their ordinary ones which do not appear on the level of consciousness but emerge in dreams and fantasy.

Ross calls our attention to two aspects of symbols: first, their meanings are socially produced, and second, their impact is often on the unconscious levels of our psyches. That is, we are not aware of the emotional impact symbols can have upon us. At the conscious level, we may have certain ideas about symbolic monuments, such as the Gateway Arch, but there are also unconscious feelings connected to them that we harbor but do not recognize.

Another insight into the power of symbols comes from the work of Clifford Geertz. He writes in *The Interpretation of Cultures* (1973: 45):

> Thinking consists not of "happenings in the head" (though happenings there and elsewhere are necessary for it to occur) but of a traffic in what have been called by G. H. Mead and others—significant symbols—words

> for the most part but also gestures, drawings, musical sounds, mechanical devices like clocks, or natural objects like jewels—anything, in fact, that is disengaged from mere actuality and used to impose meaning upon experience. From the point of view of any particular individual, such symbols are largely given. He finds them already current in the community when he is born, and they remain, with some additions, subtractions, and partial alterations he may or may not have a hand in, in circulation when he dies.

Being an American, then, means learning about the significance and meaning of many symbolic entities—including buildings and places that are considered "iconic."

At 630 feet, the Gateway Arch is the tallest man-made monument in America—the equivalent of a building more than sixty stories high. It was designed in 1947 by the Finnish architect Eero Saarinen, who won a contest for the best design of a monument for St. Louis. He wanted to create a monument that was extremely simple in form, like the Egyptian pyramids or the Washington Monument. Constructing the Arch was an engineering triumph, since the builders had to be extremely precise so that the two ends of the Arch would meet at the top, 630 feet above ground. It is hollow and visitors can take a tram to the top, where there is an observation room.

The Arch required 900 tons of stainless steel. It cost 13 million dollars to build, which would be around 90 million dollars today. There was some controversy over the decision to use an arch for a monument since it was such an abstract form and some critics of the design said it wasn't "American."

The Gateway Arch was built to honor Thomas Jefferson and his championing of the "Louisiana Purchase," which greatly expanded America and led the way, eventually, to America's expansion to the Pacific Ocean. We have always had a sense of our "Manifest Destiny" in the United States—we wanted to have a country that extended from the Atlantic Ocean to the Pacific Ocean—and the Gateway Arch can be seen as a reflection of this belief. Now, the Arch functions not only as a symbol of the old frontier and America's westward expansion but also, since the Arch is so high tech, as a signifier of the New Frontier and America's expansion into outer space, which reached its high point when we put a man on the moon.

The fact that the monument is a simple form like an arch enables people to read all kinds of different messages into it. It might be thought of as a non-representational object that can be interpreted in many different ways. It competes, as a symbol of technological innovation and achievement, with the Seattle Space Needle, a 605 foot tower, that is Seattle's dominant symbol and which I will discuss later in the book. We see this passion for technological innovation also in the building of the Golden Gate Bridge, the Hoover Dam and, more recently, in the construction of the Cowboys Stadium in Texas. We also see this focus on new technology and innovation in the rhetoric of President Obama and many politicians, who stress our genius for innovation as the primary means of improving our economic situation.

The Gateway Arch has played an important role in the development of the tourism industry in St. Louis, and reminds us that cities now compete with one another to attract tourists and keep their citizens. St. Louis has undergone continual population loss over the past ten years, so it is not doing well as far as keeping its citizens is concerned. Cities are in the business, now, of selling themselves and to do so they need to have attractions of interest.

Tourism is the largest industry in the world and cities want tourists to visit them and spend money on food, lodging and on various attractions that the city has to offer. To attract tourists, cities need to develop a number of attractions—which explains why cities build monuments, attract sports teams, and develop other things of interest to tourists: restaurants, museums, "old towns," shopping districts, and the like. For tourists to do any sight-seeing, there must be sights to see.

The Arch itself is now a kind of logo for the city of St. Louis, just as the Empire State Building and the Statue of Liberty are signifiers of New York City. From a semiotic perspective, we can say that we swim through a river of signs and symbols whose impact upon us we seldom appreciate, and the Gateway Arch is a symbol whose full meaning escapes most people who see it, but whose impact upon St. Louis has been profound.

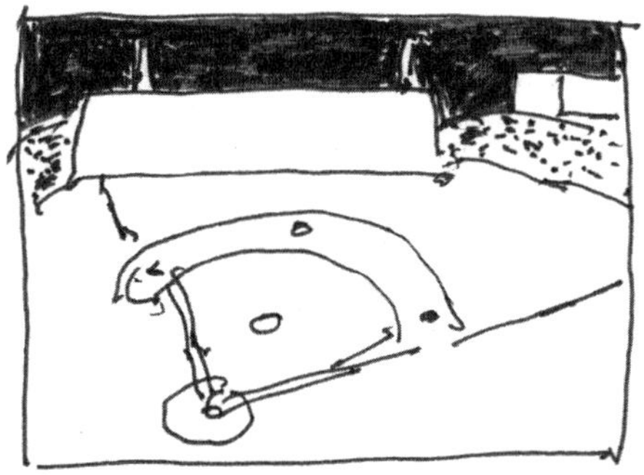

Chapter 6

Fenway Park

The sport sociologist and historian Norbert Elias analyses social structure synchronically and diachronically, coining "figuration" to designate how people inhabit social positions. The figural keys to sport are exertion, contest, codification and collective meaningfulness. They guarantee its magic attractions—tension and catharsis. Elias asks why there is such fascination with rule-governed contests between individuals and teams, an excitement and passion equal to a war but with a fraction of the devastation. He answers by tracing a trend that has fanned out vertically and horizontally from the European ruling classes since the sixteenth century. It codifies sentiment and behaviour, supplanting excess and self-laceration with temperance and auto-critique. This displacement of tension and search for ordered leisure has allocated to organized sport the task of controlling and training gentry, workers and colonists alike. High tension combined with low risk, binding popular appeal to public safety in a utilitarian calculus of time and joy.

Toby Miller and Alec McHoul,
Popular Culture and Everyday Life

The metaphor of the match, of athletic competition and battle, did not serve merely to designate the nature of the relationship one had with desires and pleasures, with their force that was always liable to turn seditious or rebellious; it also related to the preparation that enabled one to withstand such a confrontation.

Michel Foucault, *The Use of Pleasure: The History of Sexuality, Volume Two*

I grew up in Boston and spent many an afternoon in Fenway Park, watching my beloved Red Sox. Boston also had another professional baseball team, the Braves, so I had the chance to watch two of the best teams in both the American and National Leagues.

Fenway Park opened on April 12, 1912, and has the distinction of being the oldest park used in baseball and the oldest stadium used by any professional sports team in the United States. Unlike modern sports facilities, it still has a hand operated scoreboard. Fenway Park holds approximately 37,000 fans and thus is the smallest park in professional baseball. It gets its name from its location—in the Fenway area of Boston. Fenway park is also home to the distinctive "Green Monster" wall, a 37 foot tall metal wall in left field—a wall beloved by the Red Sox left fielder Ted Williams, the only player in modern times to have batted more than .400 for a year and the most celebrated and controversial Red Sox player since Babe Ruth's time. Williams hit the longest home run recorded in Fenway Park, measuring 502 feet.

The antagonism that Boston Red Sox fans (members of "The Red Sox Nation") feel towards the Yankees is also colored by the way Bostonians feel about New York. The owner of the New York Yankees spends enormous amounts of money to buy great players, which leads baseball fans in Boston—and many other cities—to feel as if he's trying to buy the World Series, and often succeeding

We can see the difference between the Red Sox and the Yankees in terms of their respective ball parks. Fenway Park was built in 1912 and the new Yankee Stadium in 2009. Fenway Park is very small, holding only 37,000 people, while Yankee Stadium is large, holding 50,000 people. Fenway Park is more intimate and more "old-fashioned." You get a particular feeling in Fenway Park, which is connected to its design and its lack of the luxury boxes found in Yankee Stadium.

Fenway Park can be considered an anachronism, a curiosity, as ball parks go, except that we find many new baseball parks have adopted a kind of retro design, which calls to mind Fenway Park. We may ask why this is the case?

I would suggest that baseball is, in essence, a nineteenth century pastoral sport. The field is much larger than the fields on which football is played, and baseball isn't as time bound as football, where time is precious. Baseball relies on coded hand gestures and the team manager wears his team's uniform, which is much different from the businessman look of football or basketball coaches.

6. *Fenway Park*

Though baseball is a nineteenth century pastoral sport, it is also a very big business that plays an important role in the world of entertainment; the televised games generate a great deal of money for teams in the larger urban areas. Professional baseball teams are big business, with high expenditures (for the star players and for ball parks) and substantial revenues, from ticket sales and advertising. The game of baseball may be a nineteenth century pastoral but the mindset of those who own sports teams is twentieth century capitalist.

Fenway Park is a kind of anachronism, a holdover from the days when baseball was often a family business and the owners had very strong personal relationships with their teams. Now, baseball seems to be dominated by MBAs studying spreadsheets and figuring out how to monetize everything they can.

But the dynamics of the game have not changed, which explains, in part, why baseball is losing popularity. Tied to the pastoral aspect of baseball is the fact that it is a game in which a lone individual—the batter—faces another lone individual—the pitcher—and his team in a battle of wills and skills. There is one player on the offense and nine players on the defense. This explains why there are so many opportunities for heroism in baseball, for the hitters bear a terrific burden and have unusual opportunities for great performances or terrible failures, especially in tight ball games. We can see here the way baseball is tied to our individualist mindset—it comes down, ultimately, to a battle between two players: a pitcher and a hitter.

In my book *Media Analysis Techniques Fourth Edition* I compared baseball and football (2012:158):

> The reason we find football so exciting is that it closely approximates and reflects the contemporary social situation in the United States. Football is a 20th-centry sport that is still relevant in the 21st-century, where we live in a world in which time is precious (time is money), communication is important (we live in an "information" society), and bureaucratic entities are dominant (corporations, universities, and so on). Baseball, on the other hand, is a 19th-century pastoral sport in which time is irrelevant, specialization is not crucial, and there is relatively little reliance on plays and communication.

I offered a chart that contrasted football and baseball in terms of various aspects of each game, which I now reproduce:

Football	**Baseball**
Urban	Pastoral
Educated players	Country boys
Time precious	Time not important
Specialized	Generalized
Body contact important	Body contact minimal
Team effort	Individualistic
Upsets critical	No upsets
Vicarious excitement	Relaxation mostly
Weekly	Daily (almost)
Two halves	Nine innings uninterrupted
Calculation, planning	Relatively little calculation
Body a weapon	Bat a weapon
Small area	Large area
Twentieth century	Nineteenthcentury
Territorial	Not concerned with territory
Team on offense	One player at a time on offense

Table 6.1 Contrasting Football and Baseball

I wrote my analysis of baseball in 1982, in the first edition of the book, and over the years some things have changed in the game. For example, baseball now is full of "country boys" from the Caribbean and Japanese players as well as Americans, many of whom have played baseball in college.

And the analysis contains some overgeneralizations about tactics and other topics, but it does, generally speaking, help us understand why baseball seems to be diminishing in importance in the American sports world. For many fans, baseball is too slow, too "boring," and lacks the physical contact and violence that Americans have come to expect and want in games. If you compare baseball with a sport like hockey, baseball creeps along very slowly and is relatively tame. The increased popularity of football in America is a reflection of the fact that Americans seem to prefer violent sports and ones that are more in keeping with our hopped-up, electronic, postmodern sensibilities. Football coaches all wear earphones and microphones that connect them with coaches high up in boxes who can offer suggestions for offensive plays and defensive formations. The fact that baseball is losing popularity is, I would suggest, a testimonial to the impact of a postmodern sensibility on the American public.

Watching the Red Sox in Fenway Park represents, psychoanalytically speaking, a form of personal and cultural regression in the service of our egos. When we are young, many American males play baseball, which explains why baseball still has a following: it allows us to regress to our childhood and the days when we were innocent and love was unconditional.

Baseball games can be boring, when for example a team builds a huge lead with just a few innings left to play. But baseball also can, at times, be extremely exciting and full of almost unbearable and painful tension in situations where the outcome of a game depends upon the battle between a hitter and a pitcher. This battle becomes more exciting when there is a runner on base who may steal second or third, or even home.

The sense of relief Red Sox fans feel when they win a game or sadness they feel when the Red Sox lose a game is mitigated by the fact that there are so many games in a season, so, until the end of the season, when winning a game may determine whether the Red Sox win the pennant or can compete for the World Series, winning or losing a particular game isn't that important.

When the sun is shining in Boston, and the weather is pleasant, watching the Red Sox play at Fenway Park is a wonderful way to spend an afternoon, especially if the Red Sox pitchers have their "stuff" and the Red Sox superstars are hitting well. If the Red Sox pitchers don't have their stuff and the Red Sox hitters aren't hitting, the experience isn't as much fun—if you're a Red Sox fan, that is. But however well the Red Sox are playing, the sun, the blue sky, the green grass, the rather intimate design of the park—all of these are signs that help generate pleasurable feelings in people who attend games in Fenway Park.

Chapter 7

The Mall of America

Since opening its doors in 1992, Mall of America revolutionized the shopping experience and became a leader in retail and entertainment.... Mall of America has been described as a city within a city. Along with an extensive range of retail, restaurants and entertainment, there are many unique features to Mall of America likely to be found in any community.

www. MallofAmerica.com

Malls have been very effective as commercial spaces. They account for over half of all retailing sales in the United States. In many metropolitan areas, competition from malls has been so severe that they have forced downtown shopping districts out of existence. Buffalo, New York, for example, has several large suburban malls ringing the central city, but the last large department store located downtown closed in 1995. During the 1960s, suburbanization and mall development were so devastating to central cities that they required large infusions of cash from federal government renewal programs to float schemes that would bring customers back downtown. Few of these efforts were successful. Despite their commercial accomplishments, malls are now locked in fierce competition with each other, because customers can commute to a variety of alternatives. As a result, owners have resorted to thematic appeals in both the design of the mall and its advertising to attract business.

Mark Gottdiener, *The Theming of America: Dreams, Visions and Commercial Spaces*

The statistics about Mall of America (it disposes of a "the") are astounding. On its Website it lists some interesting numbers:

.57 miles of walkways around one level

8 acres of skylights

4 out of 10 visitors to Mall of America are tourists

4.3 miles of total store front footage

25 rides and attractions in Nickelodeon Universe

350+ events are held at Mall of America each year

11,000 year round employees

12,550 parking spaces

4.2 million square feet of gross building area

40 million visitors annually

$650 million to build

To these figures we can add more than 400 shops, four anchor department stores, a 14 screen movie complex, and countless restaurants in the mall itself and in its amusement park. It is five times as large as Red Square in Moscow and as large as 88 football fields.

The fact that it calls itself "Mall of America" suggests its sense of its importance in American society and consumer culture. Semiotically speaking, its name suggests its national significance—a mall for all Americans, and anyone else who would like to shop there. And the statistics about the number of people who visit it, and the fact that many of them are tourists, mean that it is an important American tourist attraction and an icon with significant cultural resonance. For foreign tourists, there are shopping packages to the mall: these packages include a flight, a stay in a hotel, and time to shop in the mall. Numerous studies of tourism have indicated that shopping and entertainment are two of the most important parts of the tourist experience, so the Mall of America has united shopping, entertainment, and tourism in a successful manner.

I see the Mall of America as a kind of Disneyland in reverse. Disneyland is an entertainment venue, a theme park that has redefined the shopping experience in the United States. The Mall of America puts shopping first, but also adds a theme park, Nickelodeon Universe, and continual entertainment. The Mall of America has 350 events a year, which means just about every day some kind of an entertainment event is going on. In Disneyland, the desire for entertainment lures people to visit the theme park, where they also have the opportunity to do some shopping. In Mall of America, shopping leads people to visit it but it also provides entertainment. Shopping, we must realize, has become aestheticized in modern society and has become an important form of entertainment.

Although the mall is owned by Middle Eastern immigrants to Canada, the symbology of Mall of America can be described as American "patriotic." It has four main areas that try to simulate such areas as "main street" in a typical town, a European "old-style" marketplace, a third area that attempts to be the "Rodeo Drive" of the Twin Cities (Minneapolis and St. Paul), and a fourth area, East Broadway, that lacks a discrete identity.

In his discussion of Mall of America, the sociologist Mark Gottdiener writes (1997: 89–90):

> Despite its sometimes overreaching metaphors that try to connect with urban spaces in real cities, this mall's décor is only a thinly veiled disguise for what is an immense indoor commercial shopping area. This is true of other malls, too. The grand themed environment of the mall functions as a sign vehicle that aids its role as a container of many commercial enterprises because it is also attractive as a desirable destination. What makes the Mall of America different are its large scale and overabundance of family entertainment opportunities, including the 7-acre theme park. It represents a consummate linkage between retailing and the effort to attract and entertain families in competition with the downtown of the city, which has little family entertainment opportunities, including the 7 acre theme park.

What the developers of Mall of America recognized, Gottdiener points out, was that shoppers want to be entertained while they shop, that they want shopping to be a kind of pleasurable experience that has dimensions beyond the matter of purchasing things.

Shopping has been transformed from a search for things we need (though that still is the case for many things we buy) to a search for pleasure and a means of coping with anxieties we have. That is why many people describe shopping as "retail therapy." In postmodern societies, we thirst for experiences of all kinds and this desire helps shape our economy. The Mall of America, then, provides us with two kinds of pleasure: shopping that has been turned into entertainment, and entertainment itself.

A German Marxist theorist, Wolfgang Fritz Haug, suggests that we should see shopping as a kind of theater. He writes, in his book *Critique of*

Commodity Aesthetics: Appearance, Sexuality and Advertising in Capitalist Society (1971:69):

> The exhibition of commodities, their inspection, the act of purchase, and all the associated moments, are integrated into the concept of one theatrical total work of art which plays upon the public's willingness to buy. Thus the salesroom is designed as a stage, purpose built to convey entertainment to its audience that will stimulate a heightened desire to spend.

The aestheticization of shopping is part of the development of a strategy that makes the salesroom a theater and shopping a kind of pleasing drama in which the shopper is the star. Some culture theorists have argued that people now have so much stuff that they want to spend their money on experiences that will enrich them. Foreign travel is a good example of this kind of search for enrichment. Of course, one of the main things people do when they travel abroad is shop.

On October 3, 2003, Daniel Henninger wrote an article in the *Wall Street Journal,* "Mall of America Still Home for Shop 'til You Drop," in his Wonderland column. He wrote that for shoppers it is a Mecca—he describes it as a "retail holy land"—and for culture critics it is seen as a kind of hell. Henninger's use of language suggests that there is a subliminal religious dimension to shopping. These malls also now face competition from big box stores such as Home Depot, Wal-Mart, and Target and newly revitalized department stores.

Some culture critics see the mall as a symbol of bourgeois capitalism that exploits the masses and distracts them from recognizing their exploitation by turning their attention away from their political domination to personal consumption. The French sociologist Jean Baudrillard's attack on malls is striking for its ferocity. He discusses a French Mall, Parly 2, and writes in his book *The Consumer Society: Myths & Structures* (1970/1998:29–30):

> We are here at the heart of consumption as total organization of everyday life, total homogenization, where everything is taken over and superseded in the easy and translucidity of an abstract "happiness," defined solely by the resolution of tensions. The drugstore writ large in the form of the shopping centre, the city of the future, in the *sublimate* of all real life, of all objective social life, in which not only work and money disappear, but also the seasons, those distant vestiges of a cycle which has at last also been homogenized! Work, leisure, nature and culture: all these things which were once dispersed, which once generated anxiety and complexity in real

> life, in our "anarchic and archaic towns and cities," all these sundered activities, these activities which were more or less irreducible one to another, are now at last mixed and blended, climatized and homogenized in the same sweeping vista of perpetual shopping. All are now rendered sexless in the same hermaphroditic ambience of fashion! All at last *digested* and turned into the same homogenized faecal matter.

Baudrillard focuses his attention on the way shopping malls tend to separate us from the seasons and from all that is distinctive and human, giving us, instead, climate-controlled and culturally homogenized total environments. At the end, what you get, he suggests, is something like excrement—that is, a homogenized culture devoid of real individuality, vitality and life. We don't even use cash anymore, since it is easier to use credit cards and psychoanalytically speaking, as Freud suggests, money is feces. In his article "Character and Anal Eroticism," written in 1908, Freud explains, "Wherever archaic modes of thought predominate or have persisted—in ancient civilizations, in myth, fairy-tale and superstition, in unconscious thoughts and dreams, and in the neuroses—money comes into the closest relation with excrement." From Baudrillard's perspective, and he is not alone in his critique of shopping centers, they are dangerous and dehumanizing.

What, we might ask, would Baudrillard have made of the Mall of America, with its 4.2 million square feet of climatized shopping? And what would he have made of the South China Mall in Dongguan, China with its 7.1 million square feet of shopping space? Or the Golden Reason Shopping Mall in Beijing, China, with its 6 million square feet of shopping space? These malls are much larger than the Mall of America, so for critics of all that shopping malls represent about a culture, we must say the same in spades for the malls in China and other countries with gigantic malls. Four of the ten largest malls in the world are located in China. What does China's embrace of gigantic shopping malls say about it?

These shopping malls can be seen as symbols of a pressure towards homogeneity and conformity that have become linked to a passion to possess the good things of the world and, it would seem, not much concern about what kind of damage, if that is the correct word, these malls are doing to our souls. The shopping mall phenomenon can be seen as an example of the way modern capitalism uses against us our desire to have good things and to have pleasurable experiences. While our institutions in America are in a state of decay and our infrastructure is falling apart, large numbers of people focus all their attention on their desires for the latest cell phone or tablet or name-brand purse—whatever it is that is "hot." They resist paying taxes to fund expenditures for social consumption—by which I mean investment, building infrastructure and supporting our most important institutions—because their focus on personal consumption has destroyed any sense of social obligation.

Chapter 8

The Grand Canyon

Leave it as it is. You cannot improve on it. The ages have been at work on it, and only man can mar it. What you can do is to keep it for your children...and for all who come after you as the one great site which every American...should see.

Theodore Roosevelt, May 6, 1903, on a visit to the Grand Canyon

What may seem at face value a preserved national environment is, instead, as Raymond Williams points out, "from a whole possible area of past and present, certain meanings and practices are chosen for emphasis [and] certain other means and practices are neglected or excluded." National Parks and their surrounding regions exemplify how the forces of tourism are often centered in the manufacturing of cultural images, regions, and people that reveal political, historical, social and economic relationships among culture, state, and class-based forces of representational power. "Why are certain practices singled out as cultural traditions while others are forgotten or ignored?" asks Wai-Teng Leong. "Who, in particular, links people and practices to the past, and for what purpose? Which group is able to impose its vision of the past on other groups and why?"

Mark Neumann, *On the Rim: Looking for the Grand Canyon*

For Teddy Roosevelt, the Grand Canyon occupied a special place in American culture—he believed it was the "one place" that every American should see. The Grand Canyon is, according to a report published by *Forbes* magazine, the twentieth most popular tourist site in the United States. Most of our popular tourist sites are monuments, buildings or areas of cities, such as Coney Island or the Las Vegas Strip. There are only a few natural sites in the Forbes list such as: Niagara Falls (number eight) and the Great Smoky Mountains National Park (number nine).

We must recognize that the way we perceive the Grand Canyon is the result of various narratives to which we are exposed that offer us a repertoire of ideas and feelings that we bring to the Grand Canyon when we visit it. That is, our views of the Grand Canyon are socially constructed and like the other icons discussed in this book, shaped in large measure by historical events and the mass media. This point is made by Mark Neumann who writes, in his book *On the Rim: Looking for the Grand Canyon* (1999:5–6):

> "The world's landscapes are but the screen on which the past, present, and anticipated cosmic vanity of mankind is written," notes James M. Houston. "Land is the palimpsest of human needs, desires, meaning, greed and fears." Houston's metaphor of "written" landscapes invites us to consider how natural parks like the Grand Canyon are also symbolically constructed from a variety of narratives telling stories of American nationalism, the majesty of nature, cultural identity, the dramas of western expansion.

What Neumann suggests is that the history, the back story, of the Grand Canyon colors our perception of it.

When we visit the Grand Canyon we already have certain hopes and expectations about what kind of an experience it will be—colored, in part, by images of it we have seen on television and in magazines and newspapers, descriptions of how awesome it is and other matters like that.

American attitudes towards nature are of particular importance. They are expressed beautifully in Ralph Waldo Emerson's 1883 poem "America, My Country." Let me quote some lines from it:

8. *The Grand Canyon*

AMERICA, MY COUNTRY

Land without history, land lying all
In the plain daylight of the temperate zone,
Thy plain acts
Without exaggeration done in day;
Thy interests contested by their manifold good sense.
In their own clothes without the ornament
Of bannered army harnessed in uniform.
Land where—and 'tis in Europe counted a reproach
Where man asks questions for which man was made.
Land without nobility, or wigs, or debt,
No castles, no cathedrals, and no kings.
Land of the forest.

In the United States, we contrast ourselves (we did, in earlier times and to some extent still do so to this day) with Europe and its castles, cathedrals, kings, nobility, and ancient institutions. Many novels by Henry James, one of our greatest writers, deal with encounters between innocent (natural) Americans and corrupt Europeans. The hero of James's novel, *The American,* is named Christopher Newman (Christ, the new man).

We no longer are without debt, and our culture has been profoundly affected by immigration from many different countries, but we still see ourselves as new people in what political scientist Seymour Martin Lipset called "the first new nation."

It is a bit of a simplification to suggest that Americans go to Europe to see kings, castles and cathedrals, that is, historical sites, and that Europeans come to America to experience nature. But there is an element of truth to the generalization. People from other countries, with lots of history, come to America to see nature: our redwood trees, the Grand Canyon and our other natural wonders. Many international visitors who come to see Las Vegas, Hollywood's Walk of Fame and New Orleans also make it a point to see some natural wonders in the United States like the Grand Canyon.

Our attitudes toward nature are an important component of our national identity. Returning to Emerson's poem, we can contrast the way we Americans used to see ourselves and the way we used to see Europe, for many of us the "mother country." It would be well to keep in mind

Saussure's discussion of concepts here. He wrote in his *Course in General Linguistics* (1966:117) that "concepts are purely differential and defined not by their positive content but negatively by their relations with the other terms of the system." If Seven-Up is an un-cola, we can say that Americans are un-Europeans.

America	**Europe**
Nature	History
Forests	Castles, Cathedrals
The Cowboy	The Cavalier
The Frontier	Institutions (Church, Nobility)
Freedom	Despotism
Innocence	Guilt
Hope	Memory
Willpower	Class Conflict
Individualism	Conformity
Agrarian	Industrial
Achievement	Ascription
Equality	Hierarchy
Common man and woman	Elites
Classless (all middle-class)	Class-bound
Nature foods	Gourmet cooking
The Sacred	The Profane

Table 8.1 The Nature-History Polarity in the American Mind

This set of oppositions may be a bit simplistic but I think it reflects a sense Americans had, and still have, about how we differ from Europeans and people in many other countries. We see ourselves as egalitarians—in part, because we never had a hereditary nobility here, though the idea that we are classless has been shown to be incorrect. We have economic and political elites, but these elites aren't formally recognized the way elites are in countries with aristocracies. No nobility, except in economic realms, where elites tend to maintain their wealthy status over many generations.

And we see ourselves living in a sacred state because we believe we live in nature while Europeans and others, with history and long-standing institutions, live in a historical and therefore profane state. The American Dream, for example, is based on the notion that if people have enough willpower, they must succeed. These values are reflected in the Horatio Alger stories that were popular for many years in which poor but honest boys with "luck, pluck and virtue" always succeeded. We see ourselves as individualists and contrast ourselves with a class-bound Europe, controlled by elites. "No kings, no cathedrals," writes Emerson, "land of the forest." In the minds of many Americans, the small-towns and suburbs are where you find the real Americans, for it is commonly believed that our cities now resemble European ones.

Our reverence for nature would suggest that we are an advanced country when it comes to environmental matters, but that is not the case, by any means. In a report issued by the Yale Center for Environmental Law and Policy and the Center for International Earth Science Information Network, on the greenest countries, the United States ranked sixty-first, behind countries such as France (seventh), the UK (fourteenth), Germany (seventeenth) and Italy (eighteenth). The report is available at http://epi.yale.edu.

It is the mindset on the left hand side of the set of oppositions I discussed above that Americans bring to the Grand Canyon when they visit it. It is reasonable to suggest, then, that the Grand Canyon that Americans see is not the same as the Grand Canyon that visitors from other countries see, since our views of nature are informed by the way we contrast ourselves with other countries.

Chapter 9

The Golden Gate Bridge

The Golden Gate Bridge is unquestionably an American icon whose symbolic power rivals that of the Empire State Building or Statue of Liberty, through its representation of optimism, a distinctly American trait. Its visual linkage of form and nature, purpose and design, does not mark a boundary but instead symbolizes Western opportunities and Pacific possibilities.

Donald MacDonald and Ira Nadel, *Golden Gate Bridge: History and Design of an Icon*

More than 100,000 cars cross over the bridge daily, or about 40 million annually. It is reportedly the most photographed man-made structure in the world.

But this colossal edifice has another, darker side. Arguably the most beautiful bridge in the world, it is also the most lethal. The Golden Gate Bridge is the number one suicide site in the world.

Mel Baustein, M.D., and Anne Fleming, M.D., M.S., "Suicide From the Golden Gate Bridge"

The Golden Gate Bridge is the most famous bridge in the western part of America, probably the most famous bridge in the United States of America, and one of the most famous and beautiful bridges in the world. I've lived in Marin Country, which is on the other side of the Golden Gate Bridge from San Francisco, for forty years and crossed the bridge thousands of times.

Let me offer some statistics about the Golden Gate Bridge:

746 feet high (to top of towers)

120,000 vehicles a day use it

Cost to build: $35 million

Construction started January 5, 1933; opened in 1937

The bridge is a superb example of the way industrial structures can be beautiful. It is because the Golden Gate Bridge is so striking that it has been seen in such films as *Vertigo, Superman: the Movie, Star Trek IV: The Voyage Home, Dirty Harry, The Graduate, and Raiders of the Lost Ark.* It plays an important part in our popular culture, which may be another reason that it attracts tourists from all over the world, who can be seen trudging, in good weather and bad, between San Francisco and Sausalito, so they can say that they walked the length of the Golden Gate Bridge. It is probably the most distinctive signifier of San Francisco for people all over the world.

The Golden Gate Bridge also has the distinction of being the most popular site for suicides in the United States. It is, in fact, the number one site for suicides in the world. The second most popular site is in Japan, where committing suicide is looked upon differently than in America.

People who commit suicide by jumping off the Golden Gate Bridge invariably jump off the side facing San Francisco. When they jump off the bridge, it takes them about four seconds to reach the water and when they hit the water they are traveling at around seventy miles per hour. At that speed, the water is like concrete, and if they aren't killed at impact by the water, they die from hypothermia or drowning in the icy cold water. A small number of people actually survive their suicide attempts, but for most people, jumping off the bridge is fatal. Over the years it is estimated that 1,300 people have committed suicide from the Golden Gate Bridge, a rate of around 18 suicides a year or one suicide every three weeks.

There have been endless speculations about why people jump off the Golden Gate Bridge. Some theorists suggest that people come to the western "end" or edge of America and not being able to go any further west, in some kind of a self-destructive escape attempt, kill themselves. We can understand the significance of the "edge" of America matter by tying it to the Turner hypothesis. It argued that in 1890 the frontier ended and as a result of this, with no more free land available to people, American culture and character changed. In a sense, people who jump off the Golden Gate Bridge can be seen as "victims" of the closing of the Frontier, and with it, the end of our collective sense of possibility. MacDonald and Nadel, in the quotation in the epigraph to this chapter, suggest that the bridge symbolizes opportunity and possibility, but it can also suggest their opposite.

It may be that jumping off the bridge is a pretty secure way to kill oneself—assuming people who are committing suicide and are momentarily depressed and irrational can also think logically. Many people who try to commit suicide don't really want to succeed and their suicide attempts are actually calls for help. The problem with the Golden Gate Bridge is that a suicide attempt from it is almost always fatal.

Sociologists have speculated about the different kinds of suicides. Emile Durkheim, the father of French sociology, suggested that suicide is a form of anomic or, literally speaking, norm-less behavior. This takes place when the norms of society have broken down or are not clear. There is also egoistic suicide which can occur when people lose any sense of connection or obligation to others. And there is also altruistic suicide which occurs when people are overwhelmed by the demands of society or have a very strong sense of social obligation and are willing to die for some cause. The terrorists who make themselves into human bombs are committing altruistic suicide. The last kind of suicide is fatalistic suicide and it is caused by a sense of despair and hopelessness, which probably accounts for most of the suicides from the Golden Gate Bridge.

We may also consider the people who commit suicide from the Golden Gate Bridge in terms of another matter, what we might call the aesthetics of suicide. Killing oneself by jumping off the Golden Gate Bridge can be seen as a kind of self-destructive grand gesture in which the people who commit suicide become part of the history of a beautiful bridge. There are many other bridges one can jump off, but jumping off the Golden Gate Bridge is, whatever else it may be, a testimonial to a sense of style and to the legendary status of the bridge.

Because it is so beautiful and so famous, the Golden Gate Bridge attracts people from all over the world—including those who wish to commit suicide, though most of the people who jump off the Golden

Gate Bridge come from areas near San Francisco. There is an irony here. Bridges exist to connect places, and it is quite likely that many of the people who commit suicide have so few connections with others that they feel free to act in such a self-destructive manner.

It is possible to see the Golden Gate Bridge as the polar opposite of the Statue of Liberty. The Statue of Liberty represents optimism and faith in the possibility of living the good life in a free society. The Statue of Liberty was, for the millions of immigrants from Europe who saw it when they came to the United States, a signifier of the future, of freedom and possibility. They landed at what was for them the "beginning" edge of the United States and had the rest of the country to explore. For these immigrants, the American frontier still existed. California, on the other hand, represents the "end" of the continental United States and for some, the end of their sense of possibility.

The Golden Gate Bridge, we can see, is a complex icon with many different meanings to people. For most people it is a beautiful structure and a signifier of San Francisco and everything that is connected to the way we think about the city. But it also has another and darker significance as a magnet for disturbed people who are drawn to it in much the same way that moths are drawn to burning candles.

Chapter 10

The Las Vegas Strip

Passing through Las Vegas is Route 91, the archetype of the commercial strip, the phenomenon at its purest and most intense. We believe careful documentation and analysis of its physical form is as important to architects and urbanists today as were the studies of medieval Europe and ancient Rome to earlier generations....

Signs in Las Vegas use mixed media—words, pictures and sculpture—to persuade and inform. A sign is contradictorily for day and night. The same sign works as polychromic sculpture in the sun and as black silhouette against the sun; at night it is a source of light. It revolves by day and becomes a play of lights at night. It contains scales for close up and distance.... Day is negated inside the casinos and night negated on the Strip. The signs are, contradictorily, for day and *night.*

Robert Venturi, Steven Izenour and Denise Scott Brown, *Learning from Las Vegas: Revised Edition: On Forgotten Symbolism of Architectural Form*

As Venturi and associates have pointed out, competition in thematic displays always leads to larger and more spectacular signs. This is certainly the case in recent years as casinos have shifted to staged productions, simulations, and other spectacular forms such as theme parks and immense statues like the sphinx in front of the Luxor and the lion entrance to the MGM Grand. Such intense competition over themes has also produced a new Las Vegas experience centered, not on the exterior play of fantasy differences among casinos, but within the constructed space itself.

Mark Gottdiener, *The Theming of America: Visions, Dreams and Commercial Spaces*

Las Vegas has the distinction of being the second most popular tourist attraction in the United States. Its hotel occupancy rate is very high: 81.5 percent compared to Orlando (home of Disneyworld) at 60.7 percent and Chicago at 56.6 percent. Las Vegas is exceeded only, in popularity for tourists—both foreign and domestic—by Times Square. But New York City has eight million inhabitants and around forty-five million visitors in a given year and Las Vegas has 550,000 inhabitants in Nevada, a state with a total population of 2,500,000 people.

The fact that Las Vegas attracts more than thirty-six million visitors a year is a testimonial to the Strip's awesome drawing power, and, psychoanalytically speaking, to our desire to escape the constraints of our superegos and free our ids to enjoy various pleasures—because we believe that "what happens in Las Vegas stays in Las Vegas."

There is, we have been told, a lot to learn from Las Vegas. Robert Venturi, Steven Izenour and Denise Scott Brown describe the strip as follows in their book *Learning from Las Vegas* (1977:20):

> The image of the commercial strip is chaos. The order in this landscape is not obvious...the continuous highway itself and its systems for turning are absolutely consistent...the median strip accommodates the U-turns necessary to a vehicular promenade for casino crawling as well as left turns onto the local street pattern that the Strip intercepts.

Las Vegas may have a lot to teach architects and urbanists, but its claim to fame is that it is a city devoted to gambling (now called gaming to give itself a bit of respectability), a city that is full of hotels that are the epitome of excess (many of the earlier ones were examples of gangster chic) and a city that keeps its dirty secrets. "What happens in Las Vegas stays in Las Vegas," we are told in advertisements for the city.

In the popular imagination, Las Vegas is a classic signifier of sin, lust, and abandon, since it is a location where gambling, drugs, alcohol, and illicit sex are of central importance. It appeals to and strengthens id elements in our psyches—a matter I will discuss shortly—and has a history that involves gangsters owning and designing casinos and hotels and playing an important role in the city. Las Vegas is a city where risk dominates and where the darker elements in human beings are encouraged. And it promises you that nobody will find out what you do in Las Vegas, which loosens inhibitions and encourages behavior that is often self-destructive. Its location helps. It is in the middle of the desert away from "civilization" and can only be reached by plane or by long drives through desolate territory. Its isolation encourages the idea that it is a place where life is far removed from normal life.

The travel writer Jan Morris picked up on an aspect of Las Vegas connected to its penchant for keeping secrets. She writes about Las Vegas as "Fun City" in *Journeys* (1984:32) and sees a rather dark and sinister side to the city:

> Fun City is not funny really, after a day or two, and when the Vegas operators speak of fun, they are using double-speak. The days when the Mafia ran Vegas were Fun Days—the Good Old Days of criminals like Bugsie Malone [*sic*] and Moe Sedway—the "legendary characters" of Vegas, the "old guys." In the garden of the Flamingo Hotel, now a Hilton, an inscription facetiously suggests that its roses may flourish so brightly because Bugsie buried missing victims there; but there is nothing funny really to the hidden meanings of Las Vegas, its brutal subsoil and its often sinister compost.
>
> Sinister? The adept manipulations of brilliant businessmen? The enterprising vulgarities of Circus Circus? The tinsel of the wedding chapels? Swinging Suzy's, which features Black, English and other Exotic Escorts? Ah, but there is to the very presence of Las Vegas, I came to feel by the end of my stay, a suggestion of true evil. This is more than a discreet city, where photography is not encouraged and anonymity is respected: it is a profoundly secret one.

For Morris, beneath the glitter of Las Vegas there was a rather ugly core, and her feelings about Las Vegas captured the feelings of many people who see it not as a "fun" city but as a tragic and sad one. For Morris, the symbols of Las Vegas are the gray concrete walls that surround people's homes in Las Vegas and the bizarre agoraphobic Howard Hughes, who lived on the ninth floor of his hotel, the Desert Inn, and owned, at one time, many hotels in Las Vegas.

Las Vegas, epitomized by its famous strip and hotels/casinos can be seen as a kind of sanctuary area for gambling, promiscuous sex, entertainment (think Liberace) and, it would seem, anything else one might think of or desire. Excess, as Gottdiener points out in the epigraph, is the style on the Las Vegas strip. It also now has some of the best and most expensive restaurants in the United States. If you read Dostoevsky's novel, *The Gambler,* you can get a sense of the pathology, which Jan Morris picked up on, that lurks beneath the glittering lights and gigantic signs on the strip.

It is possible to think about gambling in terms of Sigmund Freud's analysis of the human psyche. His first analysis of the human psyche focused upon the different layers in the human mind. We can see this in the form of an iceberg floating in the sea.

CONSCIOUS
SUBCONSCIOUS

UNCONSCIOUS

Above the water we see the tip of the iceberg, which represents consciousness—what we are aware of in our minds. Just below the water is a blurry area of around six feet that represents the subconscious—material in our minds that we can bring to consciousness under the right circumstances.

But below that area, and representing around 85 percent of the iceberg, we find a dark area, the unconscious. We cannot access this dark area without help from psychologists and psychoanalysts, but the unconscious has a profound effect on our behavior. It is material buried in the unconscious of gamblers that helps explain their self-destructive behavior.

Freud later developed a second theory of the psyche that helps us understand cities like Las Vegas. He suggested that there is a battle in the human psyche between three forces: the Id, the Ego, and the Superego. These forces contend at the unconscious level.

The Id represents desire, lust, "I want it all now."

The Ego tries to mediate between the Id and the Superego, focuses on our relation to environment.

The Superego represents guilt and conscience.

The Id gives us energy, but if not controlled, we become victims of our random desires. The Superego helps guide us, but if it is too strong and dominates our Ids too much, we cannot act and have no energy. And the Ego strives to prevent either the Id or Superego from becoming dominant.

We can take Freud's typology and use its components to classify various cities:

Id	Ego	Superego
Las Vegas	Boston	Vatican City
Drives	Rationality	Guilt
Sex, Gambling	Logic	Religion

I made Boston an Ego city because it has so many colleges and universities. Education is essentially an ego function. The Vatican City is the home of the Roman Catholic Church, which, like most religions, is the source of our superego-induced sense of guilt. And it is the fact that the Las Vegas Strip is seen as a place where people can freely indulge the Id forces in their psyches that is an important part of its attraction. The fact that most of the "action" in Las Vegas happens in the evening, because it is so hot during the day, also tends to lend an aura of mystery to people's behavior there and helps them "hide" their id-dominated behavior from their egos and superegos and from the awareness of others.

Chapter 11

Waikiki Beach

Despite a generalized Anglo-Saxon longing for primitives, not just any primitives would do. Hawaiians occupied a special place in this Caucasian imagery at the end of the nineteenth century.

From the beginning, this enabling discourse of the ideal native was "raced" and "gendered" in particular ways: female, not male, and "brown," not "black," "yellow," or "red." Combined with ideologies of colonialism, these ideas can produce imaginaries that merge the feminine and the exotic....

"Woman is an island," Williamson writes, because "she is...a place to take a holiday; but she is also an island within ideology...held intact as the 'Other' within a sea of sameness.... Femininity...is a package tour of the natural."... Hawaii, as a tourist site, is still represented by the dancing hula girl.... With her dark hair, bare skin, grass skirt, and graceful gestures over swaying hips, the hula girl evokes the feminized lushness of the tropics: accessible, hospitable, beautiful, exotic, and natural.

It is the broader web of associations with Hawai'i that the tourist industry builds upon in its advertising. A destination image, as they say in the tourist industry, is the sum of all these popular associations.

Jane Desmond, *Staging Tourism: Body on Display from Waikiki to Sea World*

In the 1970s I had the good fortune to spend a month in Honolulu participating in a conference at the University of Hawaii on popular culture. The conference was organized to take advantage of our location: we did all of our work in the morning and then were free to spend our afternoons and evenings at Waikiki beach or wherever we wanted to go. I took advantage of this arrangement to spend a good deal of time at the beach in Waikiki, which has a special image in America and elsewhere as a kind of tropical paradise.

Hawaii is an American state so American tourists are comfortable there, and tourists from other countries can count on a high level of material comfort. But Hawaii is also different enough and exotic enough so that Americans feel that a trip to Hawaii is a kind of sanitized "foreign" travel, and tourists from other countries find it attractive on that count, as well. As the Desmond quotation above points out, visitors to Hawaii bring what tourism scholars call a "destination" image to Waikiki—which is the most important tourist beach on the island. That destination image is the sum total of all the things tourists have read about Waikiki, heard about Waikiki, and seen on television and films. For example, Elvis Presley made *Blue Hawaii* and *Paradise Hawaiian Style,* and there were popular television shows set in Hawaii such as *Magnum P.I.* and *Hawaii Five-0.* In 2010, *Hawaii Five-0* was brought back to television so television viewers will get more images of Waikiki and Hawaii to reinforce other images they may have picked up earlier, in movies, magazines, books, and videos.

Central to that destination image for Waikiki beach, Desmond suggests, is the hula girl. She is an "exotic" female who becomes subject to the "male gaze." This gaze, some tourist scholars suggest, is connected to colonialism and the way powerful males look at women—especially native women, and in the case of Waikiki, "brown" women. The "male gaze" can be defined as the way male tourists in foreign countries "gaze," with a sense of superiority, at native women and can be seen as a weak form of sexual tourism.

Some native Hawaiians resent the way they have been treated by the American government and by Americans, in general, and there are occasions when tourists feel the hostility of native Hawaiians, but as a rule, Hawaii is a safe and attractive tourist destination and Waikiki beach remains an important destination for many tourists to Hawaii.

Beaches have a certain role in our imagination. Think, for example, of the songs of the Beach Boys and of the curious beach subcultures that exist: epitomized by surfers with their hair dyed blonde waiting to catch the next big wave. We can say that beaches are a kind of hedonistic "sacred" space, where certain rituals connected with swimming, surfing and the whole sea-sand-sex-shopping syndrome play themselves out. Beaches are places for leisure, for enjoyment, for swimming, surfing and other forms of recreation—in a beautiful natural setting.

Surrounding Waikiki now are many very large hotels, a number of which are owned by Japanese businesses. Many Japanese get married in Hawaii because it is cheaper to get married in Hawaii than in Japan. For Japanese honeymooners Hawaii represents an inexpensive yet exotic and comfortable destination.

We can make a distinction between the exotic and everyday life. They are polar opposites. The exotic is distant and different while the everyday is near and common; the exotic is strange while the everyday is familiar; the exotic is full of people of different races and colors while the everyday is Euro-American and Caucasian, though in recent years the United States and many other countries have become much more multi-racial. The exotic involves the hut and the long house and the everyday involves the condo and the skyscraper. People who live in exotic countries often wear costumes while our everyday dress, in suits and dresses, is quite familiar.

In Hawaii dress is informal: people there wear Hawaiian shirts, muumuus, leis, sandals, and shorts and this informality is attractive to tourists. All this is important because people take vacations in search of differences from their ordinary, routine everyday lives. Waikiki beach then represents, in the popular mind, a highly desirable tourist destination: wonderful weather and the paradise-like "beach" culture that we find to be exotic, and yet in a place with all the creature comforts of contemporary American society.

An article "Royal Hawaiian Dance: How Hotels Commodified the Hula" by Molly Brush explains how the hula became a tourist attraction. The hula, she explains, was made popular by hotels on Oahu. Brush describes how a dance that originally was connected to religious worship became degraded and was turned into a tourism spectacle. It was the use of hula dancers by the Royal Hawaiian Hotel in the 1920s and in later years that played a major role in making the hula a popular culture icon. The dance met the desires of tourists in Hawaii for entertainment and for what they believed was an authentic Hawaiian experience.

In recent years, Waikiki beach has undergone urban renewal that has radically changed the hotel area around the beach, which suffered from overcrowding and petty crime. Some 7 million people visit Oahu every year, and the congestion in the small streets around Waikiki beach turned off many tourists. Now, a renewed Waikiki beach area with a shopping mall is available for tourists who want a more upscale experience.

Whether they want a more "authentic" experience is a different matter. There is reason to believe, in postmodern societies, that authentic doesn't mean much anymore. Erik Cohen discusses the problem of the growth of tourism in a world with growing "sameness." He writes in "The Changing Face of Contemporary Tourism" (2008:331–332):

> A major transformation may be underway in the West, from the modern to the post-modern tourist, or "post-tourist." While this is certainly not an all-embracing process, it may have wide-ranging effects on the nature of contemporary tourism. Resigned to the futility of a quest for authenticity in the contemporary world, the "post-tourist," instead of being concerned with the origins of supposedly "real" attractions, ironically or playfully prefers to enjoy the surfaces of often manifestly inauthentic ones. Instead of pursuing different experiences, he may choose to visit places which offer familiar ones, but in greater variety, of a higher quality, in a more agreeable ambience (or at a lower price), than those available at home. Sheer fun and enjoyment become, in this view, a culturally approved, sufficient reason for travel.

And fun and enjoyment is what a visit to Waikiki beach is all about: clean sand, warm water, cool breezes and "hot" women and men —brown, white, and every other color, and near the beach, a new shopping mall.

Some tourism scholars have suggested that visitors to Waikiki experience the "Bali Syndrome," which involves exposure to artificial Polynesian cultures and is based more on a desire for escape from the routines of everyday life than on a desire for real cultural immersion. Thus, the Polynesian Cultural Center is an exemplar of ersatz culture, with Mormons in Hawaii displaying fake Polynesian culture in outrageous theatrical extravaganzas. The Bali Syndrome would be an example of the kind of experience postmodern post-tourist visitors to Waikiki would experience and reminds us of the roles that commercialization and simulation play in contemporary American society in places like Disneyland and the Mall of America.

Waikiki may be a real place, but it is also connected, in our imaginations, with ideas we have about tropical paradises. Thus, Waikiki beach plays upon images we have of Polynesian islands as paradises—due, in part, to the painter Paul Gauguin, who left France to live and paint on a Polynesian island. Waikiki beach can be seen, then, as an Americanized and sanitized version of the paradise-like Polynesian lifestyle that exists in our fantasies.

Chapter 12

The Space Needle

"When you see the Space Needle, you know you're in Seattle, Washington, USA." Today, the Needle is one of a handful of buildings in the world that is immediately identified with its setting.... If it were not for its private ownership, it might have been sold for scrap after the Fair, but it owners fiercely defended the Space Needle from encroachment, media scorn, and public neglect. When the Seattle Landmarks Preservation Board described the Space Needle as an official city landmark, it proclaimed "The Space Needle marks a point in history of the City of Seattle and represents American aspirations toward technological progress."

Robert Spector, *The Space Needle: Symbol of Seattle*

We stand on the edge of a New Frontier—the frontier of unfulfilled hopes and dreams, a frontier of new opportunities and beliefs in peril. Before that frontier are uncharted areas of science and space, unsolved problems of peace and war, unconquered problems of ignorance and prejudice, unanswered problems of poverty and surplus.

John F. Kennedy, *Acceptance Speech at the Democratic National Convention in Los Angeles*

The Space Needle was constructed in 1962 for the World's Fair in Seattle and attracted more than two million people at that time. It is 605 feet high (approximately the height of a sixty story building) and was, when it was built, the tallest building west of the Mississippi. It is, as Spector points out in the epigraph, a symbol of Seattle and of technological progress. The fact that the building was called the Space Needle suggests that it also functions as a symbol of Seattle's connection to space exploration.

Space is an important concept in American history and culture. The Turner thesis argues that in 1890 the American frontier ended, and that it was the frontier that helped forge American character and culture. As Frederick Jackson Turner wrote in a classic paper, presented to the American Historical Society in 1893, on "The Significance of the Frontier in American History":

> So long as free land exists, the opportunity for a competency exists and economic power secures political power. But the democracy born of free land, strong in selfishness and individualism, intolerant of administrative experience and education, and pressing individual liberty beyond its proper bounds, has its dangers as well as its benefits.

It was the free land that existed at the frontier, Turner suggested, that was the most important force in creating American society and a distinctive American character. As the United States expanded across the North American continent, people had to continually readjust the institutions they brought with them—unlike Europe, for example, which no longer had a frontier and which was dominated by ancient and very powerful institutions such as royalty, the aristocracy and the church.

As I explained in my chapter on the Grand Canyon, Americans have special feelings about nature and the role it has played in shaping our national character and what we might call the American "identity." The Europeans have "history," which means institutions like royalty and a state church, and we have "nature." Turner discusses this matter later in his essay:

> To the frontier the American intellect owes its striking characteristics. That coarseness and strength combined with acuteness and inquisitiveness; that practical, inventive turn of mind, quick to find expedients; that masterful grasp of material things, lacking in the artistic but powerful to effect great ends; that restless, nervous energy; that dominant individualism working for good and for evil, and withal that buoyancy and exuberance which comes with freedom—these are traits of the frontier.

So, according to Turner the frontier is the source of our distinctive character and our democratic institutions.

The intellectual historian Stow Persons explains Turner's ideas and his environmentalist bias in his classic study *American Minds: A History of Ideas* (1958:320–321)

> The immediate and lasting appeal of Turner's frontier regionalism was owed to the fact that it emphasized the relationship between culture and environment in a way that was characteristic of naturalistic modes of thought and reminiscent of the environmentalism of traditional liberalism. It drew upon the earlier nineteenth-century zeal for the free individual, as well as upon the insights of naturalism. Turner emphasized the impress of successive frontier environments on the social organism, resulting in new kinds of social product. As one frontier succeeded another, each more remote from Europe than its predecessor, a social evolutionary process was working to perfect the American democratic individualist. A fundamental postulate of the frontier theory was the absolute power of the environment to limit the directions or forms of social development.... It was the free land of the frontier that produced the attitudes and practices called democracy.

If the frontier was the basis of American democratic institutions and of a distinctive American character, what happens, we may ask, when the frontier ends, as Turner said it did, in 1890?

For some, the answer is outer space—the so-called new frontier, which America has been in the forefront of exploring, having landed Astronauts on the moon. John F. Kennedy alluded to the importance of the "frontier" concept in his acceptance speech at the Democratic National Convention in Los Angeles. If the pioneer was the heroic figure created by the nineteenth century American frontier, the Astronaut is the new heroic figure, created for space explorations.

Seattle was, at the time the Space Needle was built, the home of the Boeing aircraft company, which plays an important part in the space exploration research for the American government. In recent years, our fascination with outer space has faded and the money we spend on space exploration has been cut way back.

But there is a new frontier now and it may have even more profound effects on our society—the new digital world and the Internet. This digital world can be seen as a kind of electronic frontier in which the same attributes found in frontier pioneers, innovation and imagination, now play an important role, as new devices, applications, and programs are created, one more remarkable than the last, to capture our attention and change, in important ways, the way we live. It is fitting, then, that one of the most important corporations that is shaping our new digital world is Microsoft, which is also located in Washington—in Redmond, just outside Seattle.

Chapter 13

The Statue of Liberty

The Statue of Liberty Enlightening the World was a gift of friendship from the people of France to the people of the United States and is a universal symbol of freedom and democracy. The Statue of Liberty was dedicated on October 28, 1886, designated as a National Monument in 1924 and restored for her centennial on July 4, 1986....

www.nps.gov/stli/

The struggle between Liberty and Authority is the most conspicuous feature in the portions of history with which we are earliest familiar, particularly in that of Greece, Rome, and England. But in old times this contest was between subjects, or some classes of subjects, and the government. By liberty, was meant protection against the tyranny of the political rulers. The rulers were conceived (except in some of the popular governments of Greece) as in a necessarily antagonistic position to the people whom they ruled. They consisted of a governing One, or a governing tribe or caste, who derived their authority from inheritance or conquest; who, at all events, did not hold it at the pleasure of the governed, and whose supremacy men did not venture, perhaps did not desire, to contest, whatever precautions might be taken against its oppressive exercise. Their power was regarded as necessary, but also as highly dangerous; as a weapon which they would attempt to use against their subjects, no less than against external enemies.... The aim, therefore, of patriots, was to set limits to the power which the ruler should be suffered to exercise over the community; and this limitation was what they meant by liberty.

John Stuart Mill, *On Liberty*

The Statue of Liberty is one of the most widely recognized American icons. It is a colossal statue in the Greco-Roman tradition of a woman holding a torch, symbolizing enlightenment, and a tablet, symbolizing wisdom. Broken chains, symbolizing freedom, are at her feet. The Statue of Liberty is the work of a French sculptor, Frederic-Auguste Bertholdi, who collaborated with a French engineer, Gustave Eiffel, who designed the steel beams that support it. So we have an Eiffel Tower in the United States except that ours is inside the Statue of Liberty.

The Statue of Liberty is now a UNESCO World Heritage Site. We can also find Statues of Liberty in France and other countries—in part because it is such a resonant symbol of hope and freedom and the possibility of rising in the world.

The poet Emma Lazarus wrote a poem, "The New Colossus," that is part of the Statue of Liberty, engraved on a tablet on the base of the statue. Her poem reflects the sentiments the American public had about the significance of the Statue of Liberty:

THE NEW COLOSSUS

Not like the brazen giant of Greek fame,
With conquering limbs astride from land to land;
Here at our sea-washed, sunset gates shall stand
A mighty woman with a torch, whose flame
Is the imprisoned lightning, and her name
Mother of Exiles. From her beacon-hand
Glows world-wide welcome; her mild eyes command
The air-bridged harbor that twin cities frame.
"Keep ancient lands, your storied pomp!" cries she
With silent lips. "Give me your tired, your poor,
Your huddled masses yearning to breathe free,
The wretched refuse of your teeming shore.
Send these, the homeless, tempest-tost to me,
I lift my lamp beside the golden door!"

The poem offers an insight into our feelings about the role of the Statue of Liberty and our place in the family of nations. When Lazarus wrote her poem, she saw the United States as a country where "huddled masses" and "wretched refuse" in foreign lands could come and find a land with new possibilities. America, she wrote, was a place where immigrants could "breathe free" in a land where freedom from the institutions and limitations of life in Europe and the possibility of rising in the world were characteristics of American society. And it was the Statue of Liberty that welcomed millions of immigrants from Europe as the ships carrying them sailed into New York, to deposit them on Ellis Island, next to Liberty Island, which holds the statue. America was for the immigrants a land of opportunity, and it still is seen as such by many immigrants from foreign lands to this day.

The Statue of Liberty reminds us that the United States is a nation of immigrants—of people from every land who have found a way to live together in relative harmony. Except for Native Americans, everyone in the United States is here because at some time in the near or distant past, someone came here from a foreign land; sometimes, this was not of their own volition, as in the cases of enslaved Africans and indentured Chinese.

One can read American politics as a battle between those who stress the importance of liberty or freedom and those who stress the importance of equality. The American Declaration of Independence, which states "We hold that all men are created equal," is one of our foundational documents. By using the word "equal" it argued that there should be no hereditary aristocracy in the United States. There is also a suggestion of equality of opportunity, which means that success and social mobility is a function of will power and individual initiative.

In egalitarian societies, there is, in principle, a "level playing field," which means that our future is in our own hands. This notion that we can succeed if we are willing to work hard enough was the dominant theme of a series of boys stories published in the mid-nineteenth century by Horatio Alger. These stories all were formulaic "rags to riches" tales that were based on a poor boy being able to rise in the world because he had luck, pluck and virtue.

Ironically, we find now that social mobility is more possible in Europe and some other countries than the United States, where the top one percent of Americans now own ninety percent of the wealth. It is still possible for poor people to become wealthy, but it is increasingly difficult.

An article by Dan Froomkin in the October 8, 2010, "Huffington Report" offers us details on this matter:

> A new report from the Organization for Economic Co-Operation and Development (OECD) finds that social mobility between generations is dramatically lower in the U.S. than in many other developed countries.
>
> So if you want your children to climb the socioeconomic ladder higher than you did, move to Canada.
>
> The report finds the U.S. ranking well below Denmark, Australia, Norway, Finland, Canada, Sweden, Germany and Spain in terms of how freely citizens move up or down the social ladder. Only in Italy and Great Britain is the intensity of the relationship between individual and parental earnings even greater.

Wealthy families transmit their advantages to their children, and these families continue to be wealthy over generations, just as people raised in poverty continue to be poor over generations. In other words, the promise that the Statue of Liberty held for people coming to the United States—that it was a land of opportunity where poor people could rise in the world—no longer is operative to the extent it was in times past and the American Dream is now more a fantasy than a reality. In the last decades the middle class has lost income and many lower middle-class families now face the prospect of falling into poverty.

The irony of the Statue of Liberty as it relates to the United States is that the children and grandchildren of many of the "huddled masses" of Europe who came to the United States now find themselves members of another group of "huddled masses," young people and many college educated Americans who can't find jobs and face an uncertain future. The promise of equality of economic opportunity, characterized by the ability of millions of immigrants to rise in the world, told and retold in many Horatio Alger novels and symbolized by the State of Liberty, has deteriorated greatly in recent years, and the American Dream is looking more and more like a nightmare for large numbers of Americans.

The immigrants of the nineteenth and early twentieth century, who came to America from European countries, actually saw the Statue of Liberty as they sailed into New York harbor. In more recent decades, many immigrants have come from Asia and are processed on the West Coast, and many others have come from Latin American countries and African countries, so the makeup of American society is undergoing rapid change. The 2010 census reports that Hispanics are going to be a majority in California in a few decades and Hispanics represent a large and growing proportion of the population of the United States. For the non-European immigrants, the ideals represented by the Statue of Liberty, not the statue, are the important thing. The notion that the United States is a land of opportunity is what is critical and what brings them here. They probably have seen images of the Statue of Liberty, and it still stands for them as a symbol of hope and opportunity.

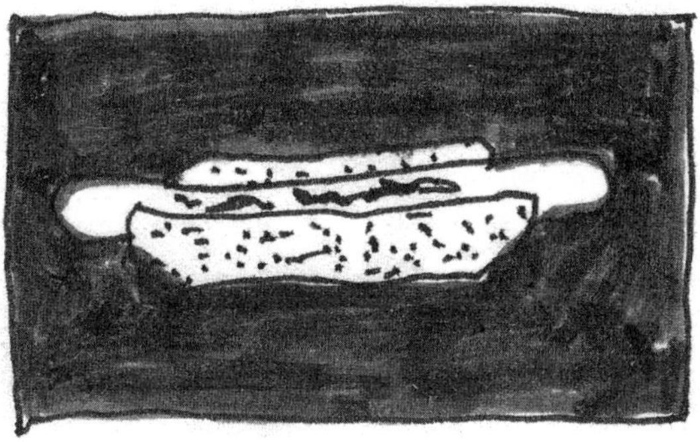

Chapter 14

Coney Island

For many visitors, Coney Island is a difficult place to comprehend and define, precisely because their memories are shaped and distorted by their overpowering visceral experience of the noise, thrills, food, and other sensual pleasures. A dip in Coney's water was a baptism, an initiation that lasted a lifetime and created a yearning to return to the Coney Island of the imagination.

Today's Coney Island, however, is confined to the mechanical attractions that occupy several square blocks.… In Coney Island: Lost and Found *I've attempted to strip away the enticements and illusions of the amusements and concentrate on the complex history of land use. I wanted to answer a common question: how was a remote sandbar transformed into the most famous resort in the world?*

Charles Denson, *Coney Island: Lost and Found*

My wife grew up in Brooklyn. When she was young, every once in a while she used to take a streetcar to Coney Island and lie on the beach—to get away from the hustle and bustle of New York. That was before Coney Island ended up as turf for street gangs in the Fifties. Coney Island is now undergoing a renewal; in its prime it had a huge amusement park and numerous places to eat, including Nathan's Famous hot dog stand that opened in 1916 and is still going strong. Every year Nathan's stages a hot dog eating contest that brings many contestants to see how many hot dogs they can eat in ten minutes. The winner, on July 4, 2011, ate sixty-two hotdogs and buns in ten minutes.

Coney Island is well known because it has been used in many films, from Indian Bollywood productions to *Annie Hall.* Coney Island was just the kind of place that inspired Walt Disney to create his own amusement park, but one quite far removed from the ambience of Coney Island, which was, in the main, a working class amusement area.

In a "First Person" interview in the October 9/10, 2010, *Financial Times*, Dick Zigun, director of the non-profit organization Coney Island USA, described what he is doing to save Coney Island. Zigun is from Connecticut and has several degrees in theater from Yale University. When he moved to Coney Island in the 1970s it was full of gangs, graffiti and burned out areas, but he could see Coney Island's potential. As Zigun explains:

> I saw that Coney Island could be a stage from which to champion art forms that had grown out of American culture: tattoos, burlesque, freak shows, things of that nature. Back then they were considered disreputable; you can study them at the PhD level now.

He set up a non-profit arts organization, Coney Island USA, and revived some popular entertainment forms such as the ten-in-one show that is, he tells us, as "scripted and specific as Elizabethan comedy. Ten strange and unusual acts rotate over an hour." He adds:

> We embraced New York City's underground sub-culture, and became a place where the new burlesque movement got going. We took it overground—if you want to blame somebody for your typical suburban teenager having a pierced tongue and tattoo, blame me.

He had to fight off developers and faced the problem that many of Coney Island's old amusements are gone, but it still has, he reminds us, Nathan's Famous hot dogs, the Wonder Wheel (a gigantic Ferris wheel), the Cyclone (a huge roller coaster), and the Parachute Jump. The odds,

Zigun adds, seem hopeless but he is optimistic because, as he put it, "Coney Island has kept its soul and is reinventing itself."

We might wonder what it is about amusement parks like Coney Island that appeals to people. The Russian cultural theorist M. M. Bakhtin offers us an answer to this question. He developed the concept of "carnivalization" to deal with the role of carnivals and popular entertainments in medieval life, when the masses sought a means of escaping from the psychological and emotional burdens imposed upon them by the church and the state. The carnivalization theory helps explain the popularity of Disneyland, except that it is so contrived and controlling a place that we only get a semblance of freedom and escape from our daily burdens. There are also elements of carnivalization in our experiences in Las Vegas, at baseball and football games, and on visits to beaches like Waikiki beach in Hawaii.

As Bakhtin writes in his book *Rabelais and His World* (1984:217–218):

> We give here a broadened meaning to the word "carnivalesque." As a special phenomenon, carnival has survived up to our time. Other manifestations of popular-festive life, related to it in style and character (as well as origin) have died out long ago or have degenerated so far as to become undistinguishable. Carnival is a well-known festivity that has been often described throughout many centuries. Even during its later development in the eighteenth and nineteenth centuries it still preserved certain fundamental traits in a quite clear, though reduced form.... We interpret it not only as carnival per se in its limited form but also as the varied popular-festive life of the Middle Ages and the Renaissance.

We can see amusement parks like Coney Island as having had their roots in the carnivalesque impulse that flowered in the Middle Ages. The original carnival periods were connected with the need for people in the Middle Ages to laugh and find some pleasure in life; present day amusement parks are connected to this need people have for festive experiences, for feasts, and for holidays.

For Mircea Eliade, a historian of religion, many of the activities of present-day people can be seen as camouflaged versions of ancient myths that shaped our behavior for thousands of years. As he explains in *The Sacred and the Profane* (1961:209):

> The majority of men "without religion" still hold to pseudo-religions and degenerated mythologies. There is nothing surprising in this, for, as we saw, profane man is the descendent of *homo religiosus* and he cannot wipe

> out his own history—that is the behavior of his religious ancestors which has made him what he is today.

That, in essence, is the point that Bakhtin makes. Much of modern day life is connected to ancient rites and rituals and, in the case of amusement parks like Coney Island, what Eliade would describe as "degenerated" forms of festive pleasures that took root in the Middle Ages.

Bakhtin also offers us an insight into why there are so many restaurants in beaches and other places where people gather to amuse themselves. These restaurants have ties to the ancient feasts that were an important part of carnivals. As he writes in *Rabelais and His World* (1984:276):

> The feast is primary, indestructible and even degenerate, but it cannot vanish.... On such days there is greater abundance in everything: food, dress, decorations. Festive greetings and good wishes are exchanged.... There are toasts, games, masquerades, laughter, pranks, and dances.... The feast means liberation from all that is utilitarian, practical. It is a temporary transfer to the utopian world. The feast cannot be reduced to any specific content (for instance to the historical event commemorated on that day); it transgresses all limited objectives. Neither can it be separated from bodily life, from the earth, nature, and the cosmos.

Eating hot dogs, pizzas and other foods at Coney Island is, we can see, an important element of the "carnivalized" experience that also is present when we attend sports games and parties. For the mostly working class and middle class people who went to Coney Island, it was a little touch of paradise that provided momentary pleasures and a respite from their daily chores and the burdens of work and everyday life.

Chapter 15

Alcatraz Prison

Alcatraz Prison in San Francisco Bay closes down and transfers its last prisoners. At it's [sic] peak period of use in [the] 1950s, "The Rock, or ""America's Devil Island," housed over 200 inmates at the maximum-security facility. Alcatraz remains an icon of American prisons for its harsh conditions and record for being inescapable. The twelve-acre rocky island, one and a half miles from San Francisco, featured the most advanced security of the time. Some of the first metal detectors were used at Alcatraz. Strict rules were enforced against the unfortunate inmates who had to do time at Alcatraz. Nearly complete silence was mandated at all times. Alcatraz was first explored by Juan Manuel de Ayala in 1775, who called it Isla de los Alcatraces (Pelicans) because of all the birds that lived there. It was sold in 1849 to the U.S. government. The first lighthouse in California was on Alcatraz. It became a Civil War fort and then a military prison in 1907. The end of its prison days did not end the Alcatraz saga. In March 1964, a group of Sioux claimed that the island belonged to them due to a 100-year-old treaty. Their claims were ignored until November 1969 when a group of eighty-nine Native Americans representing the American Indian Movement (AIM) occupied the island. They stayed there until 1971 when AIM was finally forced off the island by federal authorities. The following year, Alcatraz was added to the Golden Gate National Recreation Area. It is now open for tourism.

www.history.com/this-day-in-history/alcatraz-closes-its-doors

Alcatraz has the distinction of being the most famous prison in the United States and having the best location—in the San Francisco Bay, with a spectacular view of the San Francisco skyline—of any prison in America. It was the first super-maximum custody prison built here and was based on the theory that isolating the most dangerous and disruptive prisoners and putting them in maximum security prisons would make running ordinary prisons easier. As David A. Ward and Thomas G. Werlich explain in their essay "Alcatraz and Marion: Evaluating Super-Maximum Custody" (2000:55):

> The core idea underlying the supermax prison is that inmates, the prison itself, and the prison system of which it is part, will function better if the most assaultive and escape-prone prisoners are isolated from each other as well as from the main body of less problematic prisoners. The history of placing offenders in isolation in American prisons began in 1829, with the establishment of Eastern Penitentiary in Pennsylvania. The architectural design of this prison was intended to ensure that no prisoner could have any contact with his fellow convicts. Eastern Penitentiary was criticized for producing sickness and insanity. As the total isolation model collapsed, other strategies evolved to deal with rebellious prisoners. 'Good-time' awards and a parole system to provide incentives for good conduct were established. For short-term punishment, and incapacitation of escape artists, riot and strike leaders, and assaultive prisoners, wardens established disciplinary segregation units called 'seg,' 'solitary' or 'isolation.' In addition, some penologists argued that trouble-makers should be dispersed among different prisons to dilute their influence in populations of generally conforming prisoners.

One of the reasons Alcatraz was so famous was that it housed some of America's most dangerous and most celebrated criminals. It also claimed the honor of being escape-proof. It was opened on August 1934 and closed down on March 21, 1963, and nobody escaped from it.

Now Alcatraz has become a very popular tourist destination, with more than a million people a year visiting the island on either day or evening tours. It is one of the most important tourist attractions in San Francisco, a city that has numerous other world class tourist attractions, such as the Golden Gate Bridge and Chinatown. The question we might ask is this: why is Alcatraz such an important tourist attraction?

One way to answer this question is to suggest that tourism provides travelers with a number of gratifications that their everyday lives don't offer. I would suggest that it is Alcatraz's history, with its famous inmates (Al Capone, the Birdman, etc.) that attracts visitors. Visiting Alcatraz, also known as "the rock," is a means of participating in history by visiting places of historical interest. There is a very fine audio guide that visitors to Alcatraz can use to make their trip more memorable. People are interested in being in a famous place and seeing for themselves what it is (or was) like. Visiting an empty prison like Alcatraz is similar to visiting ancient ruins that also have historical significance. To this we can add our fascination with outlaws and criminals. Visiting Alcatraz is similar in nature to what we can describe as "disaster" tourism—the desire many tourists have to visit places where there have been terrible events that may spark in these tourists a certain kind of perverse enjoyment from seeing these places with their own eyes.

Related to participating in history is that matter of satisfying curiosity. Alcatraz was the country's most secure prison. It was closed down because it was too expensive to maintain and its design had some weaknesses, as far as controlling prisoners was concerned. One problem with maximum security prisons was that many of the inmates suffered from serious psychological problems when, for example, they were isolated from other inmates or kept in solitary confinement. People who had seen a film like *The Birdman of Alcatraz* would want to satisfy their curiosity and see what cell he occupied and get some kind of a sense of what his life was like when he was at Alcatraz.

There is also a curious matter of wanting to experience the ugly—of wanting to get a sense of what it was like for prisoners who were sent to Alcatraz. The average person spends two hours looking around Alcatraz; some tours are led by former inmates of the prison. Those two hours are enough to give tourists a sense of what spending many years at the prison might have been like.

From November 20, 1969, until June 11, 1971, a group of American Indians occupied Alcatraz and declared it as Indian territory. This occupation got the American Indians national attention for the first time in many years and led to changes in governmental policies about American Indians. The occupation generated a new sense of identity and empowerment in American Indians and a belief in the value of political activism. Many American Indians consider the occupation a turning point in their history in the twentieth century. Until the occupation, American Indians had more or less disappeared from view for most Americans. It was Alcatraz's symbolic significance that made the occupation so noteworthy.

The Indians capitalized on the mythic quality of Alcatraz and its place in the American imagination, and, in an ironic turn of events, invaded and occupied a prison rather than trying to escape from one.

Psychoanalytically speaking, we see criminals as contaminating us and our societies, and so we isolate them from ourselves as best we can and deny them the normal comforts of everyday life. Placing them on an island is the ultimate way we can isolate them. In California it costs approximately $60,000 dollars a year to keep one prisoner locked up. The money we spend on prisons is money we don't have for education and other needs, so now many people in California are thinking about ways to deal with criminals other than locking them up, at $60,000 a year, in prisons.

Chapter 16

The Cowboys Stadium in Dallas

It's a common perception that sports teams have an economic impact on a city that is tantamount to their cultural impact. This is wrong. In most circumstances, sports teams have a small positive economic effect, similar, perhaps, to the influence of a new department store.... Economic studies have shown that most public stadiums and arenas do not cover their own fixed and operating costs.... Virtually all independent economic research has confirmed a diminutive or negligible economic effect from the relocation of a sports team to a city.

Andrew Zimbalist, "The Economics of Stadiums, Team and Cities"

The Cowboys Stadium in Dallas, the home field of the Dallas Cowboys, a team that calls itself "America's team," is one of the engineering wonders of the world. It has 80,000 seats, but if you add standing room, it can hold more than 100,000 people, and once held 108,000 people (for a National Basketball Association All-Star game in February 2010). It is the largest domed stadium in the world and has a huge retractable roof. The dome is supported by a pair of 300 foot arches that span its length. The stadium cost $1.3 billion to build (much more than its original budget), has the world's largest column-free interior and the world's largest high definition television screen that measures 160 by 72 feet. In Texas, the largest state of the lower 48 states, everything is giant size, including, some have suggested, the ego of the owner of the Dallas Cowboys, Jerry Jones. His stadium was completed in May 2009.

Football is, we must recognize, a game of signs. Football coaches call signals for each play to announce offensive plays and defensive formations. These signals are codes that tell the team on offense what plays to run. Players on defense carefully watch their opponents for inadvertent "tells"—signs that indicate that a pass is to be thrown or that there will be a run. For example, defensive backs watch the eye movements of quarterbacks to determine where a pass will be thrown. Because signs can be used to lie, and signs of various kinds play such an important role in the game, we may say that football is a semiotic battle as well as a physical one.

The officials use a variety of gestures that indicate which rules have been violated or, when they hold both arms up high, imitating goal posts, that there has been a touchdown. The touchdown signal is a signifier with two meanings: triumph for the offensive team and failure for the defensive team. When this touchdown signal is given, thousands of people in the stadiums immediately erupt in cheers and thousands of others groan.

Cowboy Stadium is located in an area that had housed many low-income families, who were forced out of their houses so Jerry Jones could build his stadium. Building football stadiums for professional football teams is, we must realize, a major industry. The owners of football teams all produce reports showing how much money their stadiums will generate for the cities and counties in which they are located, but these figures tend to be wildly inflated and the stadiums generally end up costing the cities in which they are located millions of dollars.

Andrew Zimbalist, one of the most important scholars of the economics of sports stadiums, argues that sports stadiums always end up costing the cities substantial amounts of money and that the economic benefits from these stadiums are negligible. Football teams that wish to build new stadiums hold cities where they are located hostage with the threat of moving to another city if they do not get concessions. This is currently the case in San Francisco, where the San Francisco 49ers are threatening to leave San Francisco and move thirty miles south of the city to a location that will give the 49ers major concessions as far as land, highway construction and other amenities are concerned.

Professional football stadiums are particularly interesting because the average professional football team plays only eight to ten games a year in its stadium. These football stadiums may also host rock concerts, boxing matches, and other events to gain more income, but the stadiums do not make economic sense for the eight or ten days a year that they are used for football. So it is the prestige of having a professional football team that probably explains why cities are willing to be blackmailed to help construct these enormously expensive stadiums. This raises the question of what it is about football that is so important.

Every Sunday there are numerous professional football games broadcast on television, and when you watch them you see stadiums crowded with thousands and thousands of fans. Many of the people at the games have painted their faces or are wearing the jerseys of the team that they support. The teams all have beautiful young women, often in fairly revealing costumes, who act as cheerleaders. These games, then, are gigantic spectacles. (In European, Latin American and Asian countries there are also gigantic spectacles for what we call soccer and they call football.)

There are often parties and cookouts in the parking areas of the football stadiums before the game, so the game is part of a larger festive celebration and can be explained by the "carnivalization" thesis of M.M. Bakhtin, discussed earlier in the chapter on Coney Island The kind of football played in the United States is more or less unique to this country. Football is a game with so many interruptions that it is a wonderful vehicle for advertising. Here are some of the interruptions one finds in a typical game:

After each play the offensive players have a huddle.

There are also many time-outs when plays are being reviewed by officials.

Coaches and players can call time outs a certain number of times.

There is a break in the action after each touchdown.

There is a long half-time break for a show.

It turns out that in a typical three hour televised football game, one third of the broadcast is devoted to commercials. It is advertising that helps keeps professional football teams solvent, for there are huge sums paid by advertisers to the league that it distributes to various teams.

Let me offer some interesting statistics about football. The *Wall Street Journal* had someone with a stopwatch count the amount of time devoted to various aspects of the game. In a typical three hour television broadcast of a football game we find:

11 minutes of action. A typical play takes 4 seconds.

17 minutes of replays.

3 seconds devoted to cheerleaders.

67 minutes of players standing around, getting back to the huddle, lining up, etc.

60 minutes of commercials.

As I suggested in my discussion of baseball in my chapter on Fenway Park, football is a game that fits in more with contemporary electronic, time-is-precious culture than baseball. The coaches in football are all wired up and the importance of time in the game resonates with American business culture in which time is money.

The televised games have instant replay which enables viewers to see a play from many different angles. Now stadiums also have gigantic television screens so fans at the games can also see these replays—replays that are in keeping with our contemporary postmodern electronic-digital culture sensibilities. Instant replay is particularly important in the closing minutes and sometimes last seconds of a game when the outcome of the game hangs in the balance.

Professional football provides us with a remarkable spectacle. There are the stadiums full of excited fans. There are the cheerleaders dancing away. There is the vibrant green of the grass (or Astroturf) on which the game is played. There are the colorful uniforms of the players. And there are the half-time shows, often featuring famous entertainers.

A French Marxist critic, Guy Debord, discusses the importance of spectacles in capitalist countries in his book *Society of the Spectacle.* Debord sees spectacles as dominating bourgeois societies. He writes (1977:12):

> 1. In societies where modern conditions of production prevail, all of life presents itself as an immense accumulation of *spectacles.* Everything that was directly lived has moved away into representation....

> 3. The spectacle presents itself simultaneously as all of society, as part of society, and as *instrument of unification.* As a part of society it is specifically the sector which concentrates all gazing and all consciousness. Due to the very fact that this sector is *separate,* it is the common ground of the deceived gaze and of false consciousness, and unification it achieves is nothing but an official language of generalized separation.
>
> 4. The spectacle is not a collection of images, but a social relation among people mediated by images.

For Debord, the fact that spectacles play such an important role in our lives is a signifier of the degree to which capitalism has dominated our consciousness and is a means by which the ruling classes control the masses of people by creating consumer cultures and distracting them from their oppression.

Marxist critics would suggest that the intensity of our attachment to football teams is a reflection of the sense of alienation and insignificance we feel in our daily lives. We identify with certain teams and with sports heroes to escape from the sense of radical anonymity we feel in capitalist countries, they argue. Professional football is a business that exists to make money and does whatever it can to maximize its profits. Fans of the teams who purchase tickets for the games and audiences that watch televised broadcasts of the games help the owners of these teams make money.

From this perspective, Cowboys Stadium (and other football stadiums as well) can be seen as a quasi-religious iconic space, devoted to providing circuses for the masses and as a functional alternative to traditional religion. Football substitutes superstar football players for saints and complex plays for theology. The United States is the most religious country in the world as measured by weekly attendance to churches, synagogues, mosques and other such edifices. But it is doubly religious, let me suggest, for after going to church, millions of fans go to watch professional football on television or in stadiums that are analogs to churches. The players are modern versions of medieval knights in search of the Holy Grail of medieval times. Except that their Holy Grails take the form of Super Bowl rings and a lot of money.

The carving on Mount Rushmore was originally conceived as a way of supplementing the income of an agriculturally sparse land with some precious tourist dollars. By the time the planned sculpture took on a presidential cast it was no longer about money, or not only about money. Gutzon Borglum, the man who created the sculpture, took the original concept and added a thick layer of storytelling, rich with his idiosyncratic and mostly fantastical ideas about American identity and destiny. Although Rushmore invites comparisons to the monuments of the most extreme personality cults, and though personal power had an almost erotic quality for Borghlum...the monument is not meant to portray great presidents. Its official theme is territorial and political growth: "The Founding, Preservation and Expansion of the United States."

Jesse Larner, *Mount Rushmore: An Icon Reconsidered*

Chapter 17

Mount Rushmore

Mount Rushmore is clearly a shrine and repository of signification, but what exactly does it signify? President Franklin Roosevelt called it the "Shrine of Democracy." The monument can be read differently by each viewer, but in the intentions of its creators and sponsors, Mount Rushmore signifies American Values and the American Way: it transforms these intangible fictions into a somatological, visual, and consumable form. It becomes an icon, a shrine, an object of pilgrimage allowing the viewer to consume a nationalist understanding of what it means to be an American. The monument becomes a focus for American collective memory.

Michael Pretes, "Tourism and Nationalism,"
Annals of Tourism Research

Mount Rushmore contains gigantic sixty foot sculptures of the heads of four presidents—George Washington, Thomas Jefferson, Abraham Lincoln and Teddy Roosevelt—carved out of a mountain. The monument is, Jesse Larner suggests in his book, *Mount Rushmore: An Icon Reconsidered,* not really devoted to these presidents. It is, instead, a monument celebrating their role in helping expand the United States and helping its political culture evolve. Washington was the general who led the American army to victory in the Revolutionary War; Lincoln preserved the union; Jefferson was responsible for the Louisiana Purchase, and Roosevelt was a symbol of American nationalism and the expansion of the country. The official title of the monument is "Mount Rushmore National Memorial in the Black Hills."

Thus, the monument is a self-congratulatory effort that uses these presidents to make its point. It is a common practice to make heroic statues to celebrate important leaders. On a recent trip to Ukraine, I noticed statues of Lenin, often on large bases, in many cities. These were left over, no doubt, from the period when Ukraine was a part of the Union of Soviet Socialist Republics. He often is shown with a hand raised and is peering at the distant horizon. These statues pale in comparison to the sculptures on Mount Rushmore.

The article by Michael Pretes quotes an historian, G. Fite, who deals with Mount Rushmore's iconic significance as follows:

> The one who views this monument sees more than four stone faces. He sees and feels independence, freedom, justice, equality, self-reliance, individuality, and other qualities which have characterized America. (1952:235)

Pretes quotes another tourism scholar, M. Smith, who observes in his article "Hegemony and Elite Capital: the Tools of Tourism" that "monumental architecture has, for millennia, enhanced the prestige of the elite and serves as visible representations of progress, prosperity, and power" (1997:125). Smith adds, in the conclusion to his essay:

> That Mount Rushmore was created simultaneously as attraction and national shrine is clear from its history. Mount Rushmore speaks to the political guiding fictions of the United States, presenting, in gigantic and permanent form, the images of four great presidents associated with historical moments and values such as the nation's foundation, preservation, and continental and imperial expansion, and more generally with such "national" values as independence, freedom, and equality.

For Smith, Mount Rushmore, like many other tourist attractions, plays a role in the hegemonial domination of the general public by upper-class elites. It also shows the ability of elites in power to mobilize labor to honor themselves.

The term "hegemony" comes to us from an Italian Marxist, Antonio Gramsci (1891–1937), who used it to explain the way the ruling class in a society maintains its power. Gramsci distinguished between rule, which is based on power, and hegemony, which is based on cultural domination. Hegemony works not by force but by its control of culture and the ideas that shape people's consciousness. Raymond William, a prominent English Marxist, offers us an insight into the meaning of the term "hegemony." He writes in his book *Marxism and Literature* (1977:108–110):

> Hegemony is a concept which at once includes and goes beyond two powerful earlier concepts: that of "culture" as a "whole social process," in which men define and shape their whole lives; and that of "ideology," in any of its Marxist senses, in which a system of meanings and values is the expression of a particular class interest.... It is distinct in its refusal to equate consciousness with the articulate formal system which can be and ordinarily is abstracted as "ideology." It of course does not exclude the articulate and formal meanings, values and beliefs which a dominant class develops and propagates.... Hegemony is then not only the articulate upper level of "ideology," nor are its forms of control only those ordinarily seen as "manipulation" or "indoctrination." It is a whole body of practices and expectations, over the whole of living: our senses and assignments of energy, our shaping perceptions of ourselves and our world. It is a lived system of meanings and values.

Hegemony exists at a level beyond ideology and it functions by controlling our sense of what is natural, what "goes without saying." Thus, it is a very subtle means of control that, Marxists argue, helps maintain the domination of the ruling class in any society. If ideology exists at the conscious level—something we can recognize and discuss, hegemony, we may suggest, exists at the unconscious level and thus is harder to recognize. Freud's insight that material at the unconscious level shapes our behavior in important ways helps us understand the power of hegemonic domination.

For Marxists, the media are not only carriers of ideology but are also instruments of hegemonic domination in that they shape people's world views and sense of identity. The same can be said for monuments like Mount Rushmore, whose larger than life sculptures instill in American viewers a feeling of patriotism and a sense of the power and grandeur of the United States. The monument also represents a triumph of man over nature and suggests that we have the ability to shape nature to our desires. We see this also in our great engineering triumphs such as the St. Louis Gateway Arch, the Golden Gate Bridge and the Hoover Dam. Mount Rushmore (actually a facsimile of it) played an important role in the great Hitchcock film *North by Northwest,* in a more recent film *National Treasure: Book of Secrets* and also has been seen in a number of video games and comic books.

In his book *Cultural Theory: A Glossary,* Peter Brooker offers an insight into the way hegemony can be found in various aspects of a culture. He writes (1999:115):

> The idea of hegemony has directed the attention of a generation or more of academics and students to the ways in which conventional and alternative or dissident meanings can co-exist in the popular press, soap operas, a pop song, football chant, style of clothing or dance, or a whole other range of social forms and behaviours. It therefore remains a central and productive concept in the study of culture, open to further elaboration and practical work.

Brooker calls our attention to the many different forms of culture in which hegemony can be found by those who are attuned to its significance.

It is instructive to consider how leaders are honored in different countries. Over the millennia, powerful leaders have built various kinds of monuments to themselves or to national heroes. In Russia, there are statues to Lenin in all the major cities; his body is kept in Moscow in a mausoleum in Red Square and thousands of Russians and curious tourists visit it. Perhaps the most famous and long lasting monuments are the pyramids in Egypt that the Pharaohs built for themselves. In India, the emperor Shah Jahanr built the Taj Mahal to honor the memory of Mumtaz Mahal, his wife. In Asian countries, rulers often build temples to gain honor. Some rulers built enormous buildings, such as Ceausescu in Romania, who built "The House of the People" in Bucharest with an estimated 3,000 rooms. In the United States, we built the Pentagon—the largest office building in the world and a metonym for the American military services—which suggests something about the power of the military here. Whatever the case, where you find rulers with great power, they generally want to leave behind some kind of a monument to themselves.

And if they don't leave some monument behind, others create monuments to honor them.

The Mount Rushmore monument is on land that seems to have been appropriated from a Sioux tribe that owned it, a glaring example of the way American Indians have been exploited over the years by white Americans. Thus, Mount Rushmore can be seen as not only an example of hegemonic domination but also of the exercise of raw political power—to set up what started off as a money-making tourist attraction but has metamorphosed into an iconic American patriotic symbol of great power and resonance.

Chapter 18

Gold Rush Country (Columbia, California)

In January of 1848, James Marshall had a work crew camped on the American River at Coloma near Sacramento. The crew was building a saw mill for John Sutter. On the cold, clear morning of January 24, Marshall found a few tiny gold nuggets. Thus began one of the largest human migrations in history as a half-million people from around the world descended upon California in search of instant wealth.

The first printed notice of the discovery was in the March 15 issue of "The Californian" in San Francisco. Shortly after Marshall's discovery, General John Bidwell discovered gold in the Feather River and Major Pearson B. Reading found gold in the Trinity River. The Gold Rush was soon in full sway.

In 1849, quartz mining began at the Mariposa mine in Mariposa County. Gold deposits were often found inside quartz veins. In 1850, California became a state. Also that year, gold-bearing quartz was found at Gold Hill in Grass Valley. This led to the development of the great underground mines in that district and a major industry that continued for more than 100 years.

In 1851, Gold was discovered in Greenhorn Creek, Kern County. This discovery led to the rush to the upper Kern River region. By 1852, California's annual gold production reached a then all-time high of $81 million.

www.cfaes.ca.gov/ceres/calweb/geology/goldrush.html

The California Gold Rush was one of those epochal events that shaped the state and had an impact on the entire country. The Gold Rush was primarily located in the area around a number of small cities such as Grass Valley, Nevada City, Truckee and Columbia in California. Columbia was originally called Hildreth's Diggings, after Dr. Thaddeus Hildreth who discovered gold there. It later changed its name to American Camp and finally to Columbia. Most of Columbia burned down in 1854 and it was rebuilt in red brick. It is still an important tourist destination where visitors can take buggy rides and purchase mining gear to pan for gold in the Columbia State Historical Park.

Visiting the Gold Country is an exercise in nostalgia for "the good old days" (which were not so good for most people) and can be seen as a form of "time travel" that allows a momentary escape from the routines of everyday life. Tourism, whatever else it may be, has a touch of escapism that colors it.

Although some 300,000 people, from all over the world, raced to California during the Gold Rush, it is estimated that 75 percent of the people who came in search of gold were from the United States and 15 percent from Europe. That leaves 10 percent—or approximately 30,000 people—from other countries such as Mexico, Chile, Australia and China. The Gold Rush started in 1848 and ended in 1855. Many of the people who rushed to California in search of gold had no idea about how difficult it is to mine for gold and had no notion of the problems they would face in staking out their territory and living from day to day. And so they left rather quickly—disappointed and discouraged—for the promise of California did not materialize, and they left with collapsed hopes.

The American Indians who occupied the lands where the Gold Rush took place were greatly victimized. They were pushed off their land, the rivers they fished in were ruined by mining, and huge numbers of them died from diseases carried by the would-be miners. It has been estimated that 80 to 90 percent of the American Indians who were living in Gold Rush country died from smallpox, measles and other diseases. For them, the discovery of gold was a disaster. As my discussion of Mount Rushmore points out, American Indian tribes that owned the land on which Mount Rushmore was built were also victimized by powerful groups that wanted to use the land for other purposes.

It's interesting that Ralph Henry Gabriel, a Sterling Professor of History at Yale University, began his classic study, *The Course of American Democratic Thought,* 2nd Edition, with a discussion of the Gold Rush. He writes (1956:3–4):

18. *Gold Rush Country (Columbia, California)*

> In the western mountains the prospector followed the trapper. First in California and then in the broken country to the eastward, mining towns appeared. Silver City in the high Sierras reached in the 1850's a population of some ten thousand in a few weeks after the first news of the strike. For months it was a center of feverish activity. Then it vanished and its name was added to a long and growing list of mountain ghost towns. Silver City illustrates a contrast between Europe and America. In the upland hamlets of Switzerland the same families have lived for generations. There individual men are born and die, but the community goes on through decades and centuries. On the mining frontier it was normal for the individual to outlast the community. Camps formed and dissolved while the miner still lived. Those towns which, surviving the first months, persisted for a decade or more displayed again and again the same cycle of development: the high hopes of those first on the ground, the swift creation of a camp without form and without standards, the plunge into anarchy, the profits of parasitic individuals, mob violence, lynch law, and the final development of social controls.

Gabriel published his book in 1956, when things were quite different—before the development of the postmodern societies, the Internet, mobile phones, Skype, social networks and that kind of thing. But his point about the transitory quality of gold rush towns and his comparison of these towns with Swiss Hamlets (even if they don't exist now the way they did) offers us an insight into a special characteristic of California and the people who live there or move there. We might see the Gold Rush mentality as paradigmatic for the mindset of contemporary Californians.

Bill Bryson, a well known travel writer, mentioned the Gold Rush country in his book *The Lost Continent: Travels in Small-Town America.* He describes a short visit there and writes (1989:260–261):

> The towns I passed through—Tuttletown, Melones, Angels Camp—were the places where the California Gold Rush took place. In 1848, a man named James Marshall found a lump of gold at Sutter Creek, just up the road, and people went crazy. Almost overnight, 40,000 prospectors poured into the state and in a little over a decade, between 1847 and 1860, California's population went from 15,000 to nearly 400,000. Some of the towns have been preserved as they were at the time—Sonora is not too bad in this regard—but mostly there's not much to show that this was once the scene of the greatest gold rush in history.

All that remains, Bryson adds, is hamburger joints, motels and gas stations. This is because, he suggests, most of the prospectors lived in tents and left little behind when the gold ran out. In addition, many of the towns were built of wood and burned down.

The Gold Rush colored people's perceptions of California as a state for people in search of wealth, new beginnings, and opportunity. This perception of California still exists for large numbers of Americans and people from other countries as well. As a result of the Gold Rush, San Francisco became a much larger and more important city and home, eventually, to the largest Chinatown in the United States. I have a chapter on Chinatown later in the book.

Gold is a precious metal that has fascinated people for thousands of years. Sigmund Freud has an interesting theory about gold. In his article "Character and Anal Eroticism," published first in 1908, in which he deals with the unconscious significance of gold, he writes (1963:31–32):

> We know how the money which the devil gives his paramours turns to excrement after his departure, and the devil is most certainly nothing more than a personification of unconscious instinctual forces. The superstition, too, which associates the finding of treasure with defaecation is well known, and everyone is familiar with the figure of the "excretor of ducats."… Even in the early Babylon cult gold is "the excrement of Hell."… It is possible that the contrast between the most precious substance known to man and the most worthless, which he rejects as "something thrown out," has contributed to this identification of gold with faeces.

From a psychoanalytic perspective, our passion for gold, which has existed for thousands of years, remains an extremely complicated matter—one that has roots in a kind of collective unconscious desire for wealth and glory.

Gold has fascinated people for thousands of years—in part because it is scarce and therefore "precious" and in part because of its look and the fact that it can be used to make statues and ornaments and because gold leaf can be put on the cupolas of churches and other architectural features of mosques and other religious edifices. We have to recognize that the value of gold is socially constructed in western culture. For example, the ancient Egyptians had plenty of access to gold but little access to silver, so they valued silver more than gold.

These Gold Rush cities play upon our nostalgia, our wish to "participate" in history by visiting historic sites, and our desire to get a sense of what life was like in earlier times. The buildings in cities like Nevada City and Columbia have an aesthetic that contrasts with what we find in most of our modern cities and towns. One thing that city planners learned a number of years ago is that rather than tearing down old towns, it makes much more sense to spruce them up and use them as tourist attractions. Many towns and small cities in California have learned this lesson, and so these quaint "old towns" attract tourists from other states and other countries and other parts of California who wish to escape from the huge malls and the plastic new towns that pepper California.

A town like Columbia in the Gold Rush territory gives visitors an idea of what life was like many years ago and can be described as a form of collective cultural regression that helps us understand something about a historically interesting aspect of our origins. Towns like Columbia also force us to consider the credibility of the "get-rich-quick" schemes that are found in our media. For example, there are many advertisements for "can't-fail" franchises found in certain publications, and many people receive spam emails claiming that there are huge checks waiting for them. Mythically speaking, these schemes all involve magical interventions that will change our lives miraculously, the way gold rush miners thought panning for gold in California would change their lives.

Neither its rhetoric nor even the information aspect of its discourse has a decisive effect on the buyer. What the individual does respond to, on the other hand, is advertising's underlying leitmotiv of protection and gratification, the intimation that its solicitations and attempts to persuade are the sign, indecipherable at the conscious level, that somewhere is an agency . . . which has taken it upon itself to inform him of his own desires, and to foresee and rationalize these desires to his own satisfaction. He thus no more "believes" in advertising than the child believes in Father Christmas, but this in no way impedes his capacity to embrace an internalized infantile situation, and to act accordingly. Herein lies the very real effectiveness of advertising, founded on its obedience to a logic which, though not that of the conditioned reflex, is nonetheless very rigorous: a logic of belief and regression.

Jean Baudrillard, *The System of Objects*

It proposes to each of us that we transform ourselves, or our lives, by buying something more. This more, it proposes, will make us in some way richer—even though we will be poorer for having spent our money. Publicity persuades us of such a transformation by showing us people who have apparently been transformed and are, as a result, enviable. The state of being envied is what constitutes glamour. And publicity is the process of manufacturing glamour. . . . Publicity is never a celebration of pleasure-in-itself. Publicity is always about the future buyer. It offers him an image of himself made glamorous by the product or opportunity it is trying to sell.

John Berger, *Ways of Seeing*

Chapter 19

Madison Avenue

Madison Avenue in New York City was, at one time, the street where many important advertising agencies were located. It now serves, in the public mind, as a signifier for the entire advertising industry—an industry that has played an important role in the development of the American economy and in the creation of an American cultural identity. Americans are subject to an enormous amount of advertising and, because it is a glamour industry and a controversial one, we have a certain amount of curiosity about it.

There have been any number of films and television shows that have had advertising executives in them and deal with advertising, but it is a recent television series, "Mad Men," an award-winning show, that has made an interest in Madison Avenue and the advertising industry a topic of everyday conversation. The show involves a handsome advertising executive named Don Draper who is at the center of a drama about the advertising business in New York. His agency is located on Madison Avenue, hence the title "Mad Men." His job is to convince a gullible American public to buy things it shouldn't use, such as cigarettes, or doesn't need.

The series calls our attention to some major ethical problems people in the advertising industry face: what do you do when asked to help sell a product, like cigarettes, that is harmful for people? The second moral dilemma involves advertising manipulating people, or "seducing" people, and thus using them as means toward a particular end—higher sales figures and higher profits for the companies that employ the advertising agencies.

The answer that agencies that made advertisements for cigarette companies gave was "somebody will do it and it might as well be us!" That was before cigarette commercials were banned from television. The advertising agencies answer the second ethical question by arguing that they don't manipulate people but, they claim, "we only give people what they want!" A Canadian semiotician, Marcel Danesi, offers us an insight into the validity of Madison Avenue's argument that its agencies only give people what they want. As he writes in *Why It Sells: Decoding the Meaning of Brand Names, Logos, Ads, and Other Marketing and Advertising Ploys* (2008:10):

> Overall, modern-day advertising has turned shopping into a form of recreation rather than a means of acquiring essentials for daily living. It is becoming more and more an end in itself. No wonder, then, that the shopping malls are filled with thrill seekers who would otherwise

> become stir crazy. And all this has been brought about, arguably, by the type of persuasion techniques used by advertising, many of which are designed to speak indirectly to the unconscious level of the mind where the Freudian id—the unconscious part of the psyche actuated by fundamental impulses toward fulfilling instinctual needs—can be accessed unwittingly. The senses of touch and smell, which are largely downplayed in our culture, are frequently evoked in an ad text through synesthesia…so as to induce an unconscious desire for the product by sensory association.

His point is well taken. It is the way that advertising works on the unconscious elements in our psyches that affects us—often in profound ways, as the quote from John Berger in the epigraph suggests. We may tell ourselves that we are "immune" to advertising and actually believe that we make all decisions on a rational basis, but that is delusional thinking on our part.

Corporations spend a great deal of money on advertising in the United States, though as a result of the recent economic downturn, the amount spent on advertising in the past few years has decreased considerably, as the figures below show. I should point out that it is difficult to obtain accurate statistics about the size of the advertising business.

Medium	**2005 (billions)**	**2010 (billions)**
Newspapers	$ 47	$ 23
Magazines	12	9
Broadcast TV	44	36
Cable Networks	23	27
Radio	21	15
Direct Mail	55	52
Internet	12	29
Other Media	65	50
Total	$ 279	$ 241

Table 19.1 Expenditures on marketing in U.S.: 2005, 2010
(www.businessinsider.com/us-advertising-spending-by-medium-2009-10)

In 2008, according to an article in the *New York Times* about Robert Coen, the outstanding advertising researcher for the past twenty years, we spent $305 billion on advertising in the United States. The importance of advertising in the United States becomes apparent when we look at the following figures:

U.S.A.	**Rest of the World**
$305 billion	$360 billion
330 million people	6 billion people

We can see from these figures that people in the United States are exposed to an enormous amount of advertising compared to people in other countries.

In first world countries, people are exposed to more advertising than in third world countries, but the density of advertising in the United States is extraordinary. In addition to the television commercials we see we must add the radio commercials we hear, print advertisements we see in newspapers and magazines, billboards, and now the advertising on our cell phones and the Internet. The United States is a media and advertising saturated country.

Advertising has shaped our consciousness in many ways. One of the most serious critiques of advertising involves the way it exploits the female body and gives women unreal and destructive notions about themselves. In the sixties, when "Mad Men" takes place, Betty Friedan attacked advertising for suggesting that a woman's place is in the home, and since then, feminist scholars and many social scientists have attacked the way advertising portrays women as well as the way it uses and exploits children, Blacks, Latinos, and members of other ethnic, racial and gender minority groups.

One of the first and most influential studies of advertising is found in Marshall McLuhan's *The Mechanical Bride.* In this book he analyzes the first pages of newspapers, comic strips, and many print advertisements. In the introduction to the book he explains his goals as follows:

> Ours is the first age in which many thousands of the best-trained individual minds have made it a full-time business to get inside the collective public mind. To get inside in order to manipulate, exploit, control is the object now. And to generate heat not light is the intention. To keep everybody in the helpless state engendered by prolonged mental rutting is the effect of many ads and much entertainment alike. . . . The present book likewise makes few attempts to attach the very considerable currents and pressures set up around us today by the mechanical agencies of the press, radio, movies, and advertising. It does attempt to set the

> reader at the center of the revolving picture created by these affairs where he may observe the action that is in progress and in which everybody is involved. From the analysis of that action, it is hoped, many individual strategies may suggest themselves. (1951:v)

It is McLuhan's goal to help us understand how these advertisements work and what they reflect about American character and culture. *The Mechanical Bride* was not considered a success when it was first published in 1951, but in recent years it has been rediscovered and is now seen to be one of the seminal books in the field we now describe as cultural criticism, which deals, among other things, with studying media, communication and popular culture.

Madison Avenue may be seen as the epicenter from which the advertising and marketing industry spread worldwide. A French scholar, Henri Lefebvre, argues that advertising—he uses the French term "publicité" for advertising—has now taken control of our everyday lives. He writes, in his book *Everyday Life in the Modern World* (1971:105–107):

> In the second half of the twentieth century in Europe, or at any rate in France, there is *nothing*—whether object, individual or social group—that is *valued* apart from its double, the image that advertises and sanctifies it. This image *duplicates* not only an object's material, perceptible existence but desire and pleasure that it makes into fictions situation them in the land of make-believe, promising "happiness"—the happiness of being a consumer.... Thus, publicity is the poetry of Modernity, the reason and pretext for all successful displays. It takes possession of art, literature, all available signifiers and vacant signifieds; it is art and literature, it gleans the leavings of the Festival to recondition them for its own ends.... The time is past when advertising tried to condition the consumer by the repetition of slogans; today the more subtle forms of publicity represent a whole attitude to life.... You are being looked after, cared for, told how to live better, how to dress fashionably, how to decorate your house, in short how to exist.

Lefebvre directs our attention to the totalizing aspect of advertising. It has an impact on every aspect of our daily life and tells us "how to exist."

And yet, Madison Avenue's efforts (and those that are replicated in advertising agencies all over the world) are often brilliantly done and very creative, so you have to admire the aesthetic qualities of advertising, even as it attempts to take over your life. There is an interesting fact about advertising. Societies where advertising plays an important economic role tend to have dynamic and vibrant economies, so advertising may be the price we have to pay for living in modern consumer cultures.

It is the task of semiotics to help us learn how to analyze advertising by examining the signs found in them such as:

the facial expressions and body language of models,

the age, gender, ethnicity of the models,

the "look" of the models: hair style, clothes worn, props, occupations, etc.,

the use of lighting, sound and music in commercials,

the theme of the advertisement (success, envy by others, etc.),

the values reflected (patriotism, motherly love, power, etc.),

the photography,

the dialogue in commercials and textual material in print ads,

the nature of the narratives in commercials,

the arguments used to sell products and,

the role these products play in our lives.

Advertising of all kinds provides us with an incredible number of sign-rich texts that lend themselves to a semiotic analysis.

Chapter 20

The Alamo

More than 2.5 million people a year visit the 4.2 acre complex known worldwide as "The Alamo." Most come to see the old mission where a small band of Texans held out for thirteen days against the Centralist army of General Antonio López de Santa Anna. Although the Alamo fell in the early morning hours of March 6, 1836, the death of the Alamo Defenders has come to symbolize courage and sacrifice for the cause of Liberty. The memories of James Bowie, David Crockett, and William B. Travis are as powerful today as when the Texan Army under Sam Houston shouted "Remember the Alamo!" as it routed Santa Anna at the battle of San Jacinto on April 21, 1836.

www.undercovertourist.com

The Alamo as a symbol contains such intangible entities as "sacrifice" and "manifest destiny" which, according to the narratives surrounding the site, are not necessarily part of Hispanic identity. In the Texas creation mythology, the sacrifice that gives life to Texas is made almost exclusively by Anglos for the birth of a nation separated from its Mexican ties. The main role for the Hispanic within this story line is that of executioner. As a symbol for Hispanic identity, the Alamo's status is extremely negative.

Holly Beachley Brear, *Inherit the Alamo: Myth and Ritual as an American Shrine*

The Alamo is the most important tourist attraction in San Antonio, Texas, and the most important tourist attraction in the state. Often called "the cradle of Texas liberty," the Alamo played a symbolic role in the state's history and in the way it developed its sense of itself. The Alamo is also an important national symbol.

Originally, it was called the Mission San Antonio de Valero and was built in 1718. It ceased to function as a mission in 1798 and was in ruins. It had a roofless chapel that was seventy-five feet long and sixty-two feet wide and stone walls that were twenty-two feet high and four feet thick that enclosed the area around the chapel. This design meant that it could function as a fort. In the war of 1835, when Texas was part of Mexico, it was captured by Texas soldiers.

A year later, in 1836, a 5,000 man Mexican Army under General Santa Anna arrived in San Antonio and laid siege to the Alamo. It was defended by around 180 American soldiers, including Davy Crockett. General Santa Ana demanded unconditional surrender. The Americans in the Alamo refused. After a thirteen day siege, Mexican troops stormed the fort and killed all the defenders. They burned the bodies of the defenders but let the women and children who were in the Alamo during the siege live. Thus, the Alamo massacre stands, for Texans, and Americans, as a symbol of American patriots who, though greatly outnumbered, were willing to fight to the death for "liberty" and other American values.

We see this in lines in the 1960 film, *The Alamo,* spoken by John Wayne as Davy Crockett:

> Republic. I like the sound of the word. It means people can live free, talk free. Go or come, buy or sell, be drunk or sober, however they choose. Some words can give you a feeling that makes your heart warm. Republic is one of those words.

We see, then, how the Alamo's narrative lends itself to notions about democracy, liberty and freedom and how the Alamo can fit into our master narrative about America's founding and everything it stands for.

An article by Richard R. Flores, "Remembering the Alamo: Memory, Modernity and Master Symbol," makes an interesting point about the way we think about the Alamo:

> It is my contention that both the breadth of the Alamo story—its reproduction in films, literature, and folklore, and more generally its presence in the repertoire of American cultural memory—and the

> divergent understandings of it—the competing, even at times silent interpretations—are the result of its transformation from a site of defeat in 1836 into a powerfully realized and racially produced icon of American cultural memory. (2002:xiv)

What we have done, Flores suggests, is turn a terrible military defeat into a symbolic victory, making our remembrance of the Alamo a part of the American victory of San Jacinto. Thus, when we say "remember the Alamo," we are using it as a motivation for our fighting and using its memory as an instrumental part of a military victory.

The Alamo plays an important role in what might be described as the "creation myth" of the state of Texas and in American cultural mythology. The United States, using the excuse of a spurious invasion of the United States by Mexico, launched a war in 1846 that eventually led to making Texas part of the continental United States. When Flores, who is a Mexican-American anthropologist, uses the term "racial" in his analysis, he is calling our attention to the fact that our memory of the Alamo is colored by myth and serves the purposes of the dominant white Anglo-Saxon majority in Texas and in the United States.

Brear suggests that the Alamo story with its Mexican executioners is the source of tensions felt all through the United States about Mexicans (and one can add Hispanics). It is reasonable to suggest that the way many Americans in the southwest feel about Mexicans has been colored by the Alamo story that became transformed into a myth.

I deal with the way American society has treated other racial and ethnic minorities in my chapters on Waikiki Beach, on Alcatraz Prison, on Mount Rushmore and on San Francisco's Chinatown. The theme that runs through all these discussions is the way a majority white culture has exploited the relative powerlessness of racial and ethnic minorities in America. This exploitation happened when America was essentially a white, Anglo-Saxon, Protestant (WASP) country. In contemporary American society, as the result of immigration (both legal and illegal), the makeup of our society has changed, and we find ourselves living in a multi-cultural, multi-ethnic, multi-racial society, in which minorities of all kinds are increasingly assertive and have begun playing an important role in our economy and our political life.

The Alamo story functions as one of our central mythic narratives for Americans who undergo, as Brear puts it, "regeneration in the sacrificial death inside the Alamo image" and as an archetype of American regeneration that is closely connected to violence. "Remember the Alamo" is, then, a white perspective on things; from the Mexican perspective, the saying would be "Forget the Alamo." For Mexicans, the Alamo is a symbol of their exploitation and displacement by Anglos, an excuse for racism by whites, and a problem for modern Mexican-Americans who wish to play a more important role in the economic and political life of San Antonio, Texas and the United States.

Chapter 21

Graceland

Every king has a mansion. Elvis was no different. From the minute you enter the door of Graceland, you know you're on hallowed ground. The Mansion gives an intimate look into the personal life of Elvis Presley. From his humble beginnings in Tupelo, Mississippi, to his Hall of Gold records, you will see the triumphs of the King of Rock 'n' Roll. It doesn't stop there. The experience is made even more personal by the audio tour narrated by Lisa Marie and featuring audio clips of the Presley family. There are exhibits, jets, automobiles and movie memorabilia to name a few. Plan to spend some time touring the Mansion and grounds. The 13.8 acre estate was purchased by Elvis Presley in early 1957 at the age of 22. He moved from his home on Audubon Drive due to privacy and security concerns. The Graceland Mansion has 23 rooms including 8 bedrooms and bathrooms. After his purchase, Elvis made significant modifications to his home including a fieldstone wall surrounding the property, wrought-iron music-themed gate, swimming pool, racquetball court and the "Jungle Room" which features an indoor water fall. In 1982, five years after Elvis' death in 1977, the family opened Graceland Mansion for public tours. His custom jets, the Lisa Marie *and* Hound Dog II *that had previously been sold, were brought back to Graceland in 1984. Later in 1989, the Automobile Museum was opened. In 1991, Graceland was placed on the National Register of Historic Places. In 2005, it became a National Historic Landmark. Graceland Mansion has hosted millions of visitors from every state in the union and nearly every country of the world.*

Graceland has the distinction of being the second most visited private home in the United States, after the White House, which isn't only a private home. Some 600,000 to 700,000 people a year make a "pilgrimage" to Graceland, which was declared a National Historic Landmark in 2006. The description of Graceland as "hallowed ground," posted on the internet by the Memphis tourist organization, gives us a great deal to think about. Presley was known as "the King of Rock 'n' Roll" so the allusions to him as a "king" are not that far-fetched.

He was an extremely important figure in American popular culture. The composer and conductor Leonard Bernstein described Presley as "the greatest cultural force in the Twentieth Century." He sold 500 million records and made 33 films in his career. Greil Marcus, an important scholar of music and popular culture wrote about Presley as follows:

> Elvis Presley is a supreme figure in American life, one whose presence, no matter how banal or predictable, brooks no real comparisons. ... The cultural range of his music has expanded to the point where it includes not only the hits of the day, but also patriotic recitals, pure country gospel, and really dirty blues. ... Elvis has emerged as a great *artist,* a great *rocker,* a great *purveyor of schlock,* a great *heart throb,* a great *bore,* a great *symbol of potency,* a great *ham,* a great *nice person,* and, yes, a great American.

Presley had a distinctive look. He had long sideburns and wore flashy clothes and that look—semiotically speaking his distinctive signifiers—has given rise to legions of Presley imitators who style their hair the way he did, wear flashy clothes, sing his songs and keep his legend alive.

He was born on January 8, 1935, and died on August 16, 1977, at the age of forty-two from a heart attack caused, most likely, by the drugs that he took to deal with his weight problem. He was, at the time of his death, the most successful solo artist in the history of rock 'n' roll.

Presley bought Graceland when he was only 22 years old, which gives us an insight into how successful he was as a recording artist and later as a film star. Describing Graceland—and the term "grace" has an obvious religious significance—as "hallowed ground" suggests a holy or almost sacred dimension to Graceland. We can also find Christian religious overtones in many of Presley's movies that feature a young guy who is led astray by a materialistic desire for power and wealth. He eventually is "saved" by discovering the importance of ethical behavior and religious values—a theme found in many religious stories told in southern Baptist churches every Sunday.

21. *Graceland*

In addition to the religious aspects of Presley's films, it is possible to see him as a mythic figure; the events in his life closely parallel the archetypal myth of the hero, as described by Joseph L. Henderson in his essay "Ancient Myths and Modern Man." This essay appears in Carl G. Jung's book *Man and His Symbols*. In his essay, Henderson sketches out the myth of the hero. He writes (1968:101):

> The myth of the hero is the most common and best known myth in the world.... These hero myths vary enormously in detail, but the more closely one examines them the more one sees that structurally they are very similar.... Over and over again one hears a tale describing a hero's miraculous but humble birth, his early proof of superhuman strength, his rapid rise to prominence or power, his triumphant struggle with the forces of evil, his fallibility to the sin of pride (*hybris*), and his fall through betrayal or a "heroic" sacrifice that ends in his death.... In many of these stories the early weakness of the hero is balanced by the appearance of strong "tutelary" figures—or guardians—who enable him to perform the superhuman tasks that he cannot accomplish unaided.

It is easy to recognize parallels between the archetypal myth of the hero and Presley's life.

Presley's parents were poor. When he was young he went to services in fundamentalist churches where the preachers were extremely lively, trying to stir their parishioners. His parents purchased a guitar for him when he was 11, and they attended many fairs with him, where he was exposed to country music. Presley loved black music and country music and used them in forging his rockabilly style of music. To this music he added the shaking hips and body movements of some of the fundamentalist preachers he observed when he went to church.

I spell out the parallels between mythic heroes and Presley's life as follows:

The Mythic Hero	Elvis Presley
Humble birth	Parents were poor
Superhuman strength	Great musical ability
Tutelary figures	Colonel Tom Parker
Rapid rise	Bought Graceland when 22
Heroic sacrifice	Early death
Place of death important	Graceland a shrine

Table 21.1 Comparing Mythic Heroes to Elvis Presley

What audiences got with Presley's "rockabilly" performances was a white man singing black music with the hip swinging that, at the time, was seen as outrageous. When Presley appeared on the Ed Sullivan show, orders were given to the camera operators to only show him from the waist up.

We can see Colonel Tom Parker, who was a manager of country music performers, as Presley's "tutelary" figure, who guided his career. In 1956, Presley's recording of "Heartbreak Hotel" sold two million single records, and that led to national television exposure and ultimately to Presley's film career. His "heroic sacrifice" can be seen in his early death—which for his fans is seen as a kind of "sacrifice," perhaps to the gods of music. What is interesting about Presley is the way his fans have turned him into a mythic hero—much like the way John Lennon has been made into a mythic, sacrificial hero, and the way Jesus is seen by Christians as a sacrificial figure. Given the facts of Presley's life, and his early death, it is easy to understand how he has become a mythic hero and how Graceland has become a kind of shrine for everyone who loves his music and is curious about where he lived and how he lived.

In his book, *The Sacred and the Profane,* the historian of religion, Mircea Eliade, makes a distinction between sacred and profane space. He offers the example of a church. For believers, the door to a church marks the end of profane space and the beginning of sacred space—an area that partakes of holiness and is connected to the history of the Church and to attitudes believers have about the value of being in a sacred space. The same feelings we get in religious sacred space can be had in other kinds of sacred space, such as those found in patriotic sites or places that have personal meaning.

As Eliade writes (1961:24):

> There are, for example, privileged places, qualitatively different from all others—a man's birthplace, or the scenes of his first love, or certain places in the first foreign city he visited in youth. Even for the most frankly nonreligious man, all of these places still retain an exception, a unique quality; they are the "holy" places of his private universe, as if it were in such spots that he had received the revelation of a reality *other* than that in which he participates through his ordinary daily life.

We can see Graceland as having an aura of sacred space and as functioning as a shrine for Presley's millions of fans for whom he remains a mythic hero and for some, it would seem, even a god-like figure.

Construction of the Hoover Dam—the great pyramid of the American West, fount for a twentieth-century civilization—began in 1931 and was concluded in 1936. The first and most important link in a chain of dams, canals, and aqueducts built to harness the Colorado River, it was the supreme engineering feat of its day, a soul-stirring architectural and industrial achievement, the ultimate expression of machine-age America's ingenuity and technological progress. More than half a century later, the white concrete wedge on the Arizona-Nevada border still inspires awe. A new generation of bigger, more sophisticated engineering marvels has risen, yet Hoover Dam remains the benchmark, the most famous dam in the world, a monumental and distinctly American icon.

Joseph E. Stephens, *Hoover Dam: An American Adventure*

Chapter 22

The Hoover Dam

When the Hoover Dam was completed in 1936, at a cost of 49 million dollars, it was the largest dam in the world. The statistics about the dam, technically speaking a concrete arch dam, are incredible:

Cost:	$49 million
Length:	1,244 feet
Height:	726 feet
Thickness:	664 feet at base, 44 feet at top
Electricity generated:	4.2 billion kilowatts
Amount of concrete:	3,250,000 cubic yards
Number of workers:	5,000
Workers killed:	112

These statistics provide us an idea of the gigantic size of the dam and of the enormous amount of labor that went into the construction of what was, at the time, considered to be an engineering marvel. Construction started on the dam in 1930 and finished in 1936, ahead of schedule. The Hoover Dam is now an important tourist attraction, drawing a million visitors a year, many from nearby Las Vegas, thirty miles away, where a variety of tours to the dam and the Grand Canyon that can be purchased.

It was during the 1930s that the United States built the Hoover Dam, the Golden Gate Bridge, and the 102 story Empire State Building, which was the tallest building in the world until the World Trade Center was built in the 1970s. In terms of engineering triumphs, we showed the way in the 1930s and our accomplishments in outer space, many years after the thirties, showed that American ingenuity and genius were still of some consequence. America stood for infinite possibility and the American Dream—that anyone could succeed if he or she was willing to work hard enough—seemed a reality.

The dam was, for many years, the largest dam in the world. The honor now goes to the Three Gorges Dam in China, which dwarfs the Hoover Dam. To understand the size of the Three Gorges Dam, I will compare the two dams:

	Hoover	**Three Gorges**
Length:	1,244 feet	7,661 feet
Height:	726	607
Concrete used:	3,250,000 cubic yards	26,430,000 cubic yards

We can see that the Three Gorges Dam is six times as long as the Hoover Dam and has eight times as much concrete in it. We must recognize that the Hoover Dam was built in the 1930s, before many modern means of dam building developed and was, at the time, considered to be an engineering marvel.

The Hoover Dam was a signifier of America's industrial might and its leadership in engineering, technology and dam building. The Three Gorges Dam, now the largest dam in the world, can be taken as an important symbol of China's emergence in recent years as an economic superpower. The Chinese, we may say, are on the way up; the question that many Americans ask now is—are we on the way down?

Two communication scholars, Richard Rogers and Julia Kalil Schuten, have written an article on the symbolic significance of the Hoover Dam. In "The Gender of Water and the Pleasure of Alienation: A Critical Analysis of Visiting Hoover Dam" they write (2004:259):

> Through a critical reading of the educational displays, films, plaques, and other texts as well as the physical structure of the dam itself, three rhetorical strategies used in the dam's official representation are identified. First, the Bureau of Reclamation presents the Colorado River as a chaotic, feminine entity in need of masculine control. Second, the river's rhetorical status as Other encourages audiences to identify with the subject's position as nature's master and thereby participate in the pleasures such an identity offers. Third, the Bureau uses the prevalent "common sense" of Native Americans as environmentally sensitive in combination with an "historical" Native American voice to establish the dam as both environmentally sound and a logical step in humanity's progress toward economic development and domination over nature.

This theme of "feminine" wild rivers needing "masculine" control reflects the patriarchal mindset that was prevalent in what we might describe as an American masculinist culture. Before the rise of feminism in America, women were looked upon as "weak, highly emotional and therefore wild" creatures who needed the strength and rationality of men. This, of course, was sheer nonsense, and was used by men to justify the way they subordinated women, just as they subordinated and exploited ethnic, racial and religious minorities.

The Rogers and Schuten analysis uses informative material about the dam such as films and plaques as well as the experience of visiting the dam to reveal the symbolic meanings of the Hoover Dam for Americans.

They suggest that the way people react to the Hoover Dam is affected, to a considerable degree, by the way the dam has been presented to people by the government.

Their paper contends that there are certain notions about the Colorado River and the "common sense" of Native Americans that were used by the agency that creates tourist materials to give visitors to the dam a sense of its significance. In academic language, we would say that the meaning of the dam, like so many other things in life, is socially constructed. That is, tourists are, to a considerable extent, guided by films and brochures and other material to think and feel about the Hoover Dam in certain ways. There are also visceral reactions to the dam from tourists who are amazed at how huge it is. When we are in the presence of a gigantic structure like the Hoover Dam, we cannot avoid having a sense how small we are.

I would add to this analysis other things the Hoover Dam suggests. We can read the Hoover Dam as standing at a high point in America's sense of possibility. It was built during the great Depression, but the Hoover Dam, as a symbol of the great achievement of American engineers and builders, meant that Americans could sense that things would be getting better in the future. The Hoover Dam was built around the same time that Henry Ford created the Model T car and factories used the theories of FrederickTaylor to modernize and rationalize what they produced. Both of these developments suggested a better future.

That future, when the Depression's impact was ameliorated, was ten years away. It is generally recognized that it was the Second World War that enabled the United States to escape from the Depression. The country was affluent for many years, until the economic collapse of 2008, the most severe depression since the great Depression of the thirties.

The Hoover Dam was a symbol of a country on the rise, but that was a long time ago. America seems to have lost its groove, and though we are the wealthiest country in the world, we do not use our resources as well as we might. Now, it appears that the American dream has faded, and America finds itself being surpassed in many different ways by other countries. The Hoover Dam remains a remarkable feat of construction, that was considered, at the time, one of the wonders of the world. But now it is a signifier of a country that may have peaked, that is no longer as great as it once was, and that is not certain about whether it can regain its past glory.

Grauman's particular contribution was to pioneer "first-run premieres," extravagant social events that featured searchlights and red carpets, all to celebrate running a roll of celluloid through a machine. He also introduced the "prologue," a live act related to the theme of the feature film, to give people more for their money and to compete with other theatres.... Grauman's attitude was, "the public doesn't demand *anything...It is only after a thing is created that the public demands it." And he was adept at telling people what they thought they wanted. One of his stunts was the idea of having actors leave their footprints in cement in front of his Chinese Theatre. People still come to see these consecrated blocks of concrete, often without going inside to see the film. There were many apocryphal accounts of how this custom started and Grauman let all of them proliferate.*

Maggie Valentine, *The Show Starts on the Sidewalk: An Architectural History of the Movies*

Hollywood...is faced with the task of producing films that draw the masses, in particular the American masses.... The film industry is forced by its profit interest to divine the nature of actually existing mass trends and to adjust its products to them. That this necessity leaves a margin for cultural initiative on the part of the industry does not alter the situation. To be sure, American audiences receive what Hollywood wants them to want; but in the long run audience desires, acute or dormant, determine the character of Hollywood films....

Sigfried Kracauer, "National Types as Hollywood Presents Them"

Chapter 23

Grauman's Chinese Theater

Grauman's Chinese Theater is a symbol of Hollywood, film stars, glamour, and everything connected with the movie industry. It is on Hollywood Boulevard, has 2,200 seats, and is the site of the "Hollywood Walk of Fame," where actors' and actresses' signatures, footprints and handprints can be found in the patio in front of the theater. The theatre opened on May 18, 1927, with a premiere of Cecil B. DeMille's *The King of Kings,* has hosted a number of Academy Awards ceremonies, and, with its "Hollywood Walk of Fame," is now a famous tourist attraction. As one of the many Internet sites that deals with Hollywood and the film industry put it, "If you're going to make the pilgrimage to Hollywood, the Chinese Theatre is a must-see" (www.seeing-stars.com/theatres/chinesetheatre.shtml).

The Grauman Theater's ornate exterior, which replicates a Chinese Pagoda, and the red carpets and other things connected with movie stars visiting the theater, can be seen as examples of the kind of flashy and glitzy sensibility that was found in Hollywood in its earliest days. And Grauman's elaborate premieres helped establish movie stars as a kind of American royalty, our home-grown equivalent of the hereditary aristocracies found in some European countries and various Asian despotic royalties.

In her classic study, *Hollywood, the Dream Factory,* anthropologist Hortense Powdermaker analyses Hollywood based on a year spent there, interviewing people and observing the Hollywood lifestyle and the film business. In the second chapter of her book she writes (1950:39–40):

> HOLLYWOOD IS ENGAGED in the mass production of prefabricated daydreams. It tries to adapt the American dream, that all men are created equal, to the view that all men's dreams should become equal. Movies are the first popular art to become a big business with mass production and mass distribution. It is quite obvious that movies cannot be individually produced, and that some form of mass production is inevitable. But the assumption is that for any sort of mass production more than one kind of social system is possible.... A feature of all mass production is the uniformity of the menu. Hollywood has tried to achieve this by seeking formulas that it hopes will work for all movies and insure their success.... Since all members of the human species have the same basic needs and have some characteristics in common, there are certain simple forms of entertainment to which they can all respond. But now, when movies are big business, and the mass production and uniformity in the prefabricated

> daydreams more desirable to the manufacturer, such uniform products have become less salable.

Powdermaker wrote her book in 1950, so her analysis of the movie industry deals with it in its earlier days and its relation to American culture in the forties. Obviously, a great deal has changed in American society and in the film industry since then, but the dynamics are the same.

We can make a distinction in the way film scholars use the terms *film* and *movies*. They use movies for the mass entertainment works that have been popular over the years, texts that tend to be formulaic and which reflect commonly held American attitudes and values. Film, on the other hand, is used for serious works of art that are not formulaic and reflect the distinctive sensibilities of the directors who make the films. These texts are typically shown in "Art Film" theaters and are not widely popular, as a rule.

I can only wonder what Powdermaker would have written about all the movies that have been made about comic-strip characters such as Superman, Batman and Spider-Man. What is interesting about some of these movies is the way they have been turned into texts that, in many respects, reflect an art-film sensibility. Film is a narrative art form and in the comics one finds highly developed narratives. The heroes and heroines of comic strips bring an audience of readers who are familiar with these heroes. The writers of these films about comic strip characters then can take these familiar characters and create narratives that transcend the limitations of the comic strip format, and of conventional movies in some cases.

Powdermaker would probably respond to these movies the way she analyzed the ones she saw in the 1940s. Whatever genre of film one deals with, whether it is a lowbrow movie or a highbrow art film, inevitably these texts reflect the values and belief systems prevalent in the artists who make them. Generally critics focus on the director as auteur—or "author"—and the society in which the texts are made. Movies and films are useful for culture critics, who can "read" these works for insights into the cultures in which they are made and the mindset of the writers and directors who make them.

She saw a kind of totalitarianism in the film industry, where cutthroat behavior was the norm. As she writes (332):

> Hollywood has the elaborated totalitarian element we have described: the concept of people as property and as objects to be manipulated, highly

concentrated and personalized power for power's sake, an amorality, and an atmosphere of breaks, continuous anxiety and crises. The result of this is an over-elaboration in business inefficiency, deep frustration in human relations, and a high number of unentertaining second- and third-rate movies.

She also wrote that it was possible for Hollywood to popularize other values that are democratic in nature, but wasn't confident that these values would become dominant in the American film industry.

If you look at the content of popular Hollywood movies, especially ones made in earlier times, and American popular culture, you notice that they reflect dominant themes in American culture such as:

the "living happily ever after" ending,

the goodness of ordinary people,

the American Dream of inevitable success,

the redemption of a wayward person

the boy gets the girl (after losing her),

the triumph of the underdog,

the ideal nature of small town life, and

the way good wins over evil.

When people go to the movies, generally speaking, they want to see their values and beliefs reinforced and want to avoid cognitive dissonance—that is, they don't want to see their values attacked.

In recent decades, we have seen many films that are more nuanced and more complex, reflecting a more sophisticated sensibility. Postmodern films like *Blade Runner, The Terminator,* and *Crimes and Misdemeanors* are made from time to time, but we mostly have popular movies reflecting commonly accepted values.

I had the pleasure of spending a week at a conference on the film industry in Los Angeles a number of years ago sponsored by the American Film Institute. I asked a producer I met there what it felt like to spend twenty million dollars on a film; at that time, that's what films cost. He looked at me and smiled. "Think of it this way. You pour twenty million dollars into this funnel and hope that two hundred million dollars will come out the other end." Not all films make money, but nowadays there are so many different ways a film can make money (foreign sales, television showings, DVDs) that films are relatively safe investments, as a rule.

23. *Grauman's Chinese Theater*

Although we do not have a hereditary aristocracy in the United States, we do have a kind of "royalty" made up of sports and entertainment figures, especially movie stars, who live glamorous lives and whose activities are followed by millions of fans in magazines and now on the Internet. We get a sense of the special status of our American royals when there are big movie openings, such as the one held at Grauman's recently for a Harry Potter movie, with many movie stars and all the glitter that goes with these openings—fans, red carpets, security guards, and long limos.

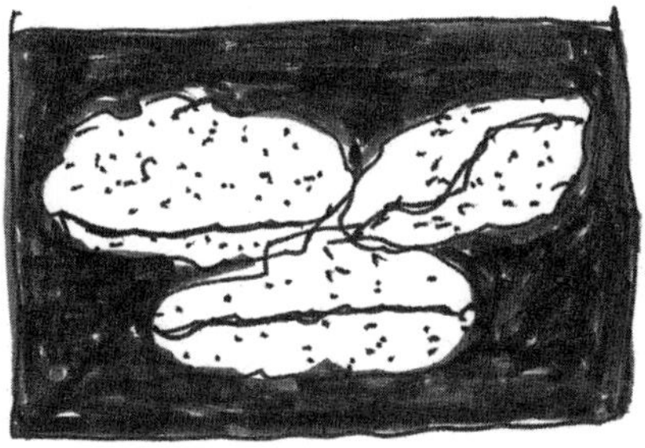

Chapter 24

The French Quarter

The French Quarter, also known as Vieux Carré—or the "Quarter" to locals—sits on a crescent in the Mississippi River on some of the highest ground in New Orleans. Not only is this the city's cultural hub, but is a community where residents take time to reminisce with neighbors about times gone by and to welcome visitors in the streets.

Intimate and unique, New Orleans' oldest neighborhood has exerted a spell over writers and artists since the time of Mark Twain, Lafcadio Hern and John James Audubon. Hollywood celebrities and software magnates have joined the residential mix, keeping the glamour up-to-date, but it is the year-round local residents who keep the neighborhood vibrant.

French Quarter architecture is a mix of Spanish, French, Creole and American styles. Plastered walls and single chimneys reflect laws enacted after fire virtually destroyed the city in 1788 and 1794. Walled courtyards, perfect for French Quarter parties, are a gift of the Spanish influence. Cast iron balconies were added to many masonry buildings after 1850, when Baroness Pontalba included them on her fashionable row houses near Jackson Square. These lacy galleries, along with plentiful stoops and porches on younger buildings, make the Quarter a great place for people-watching and every kind of person imaginable can be spotted on the sidewalks of the Quarter.

www.neworleans.com/neworleans/fq/

New Orleans is a major tourist destination in the United States, for visitors who love to wander around the French Quarter and who are attracted by the ambiance of the city, its many lively music clubs, bars and wonderful restaurants. In New Orleans one can attend a philharmonic orchestra concert, go to the ballet, attend an opera, see legitimate theater productions, go to a New Orleans Saints football game, listen to jazz in a bar, and take river cruises on the Natchez steam boat. New Orleans is one of the top ten tourism destinations in the United States, and considering its small size—around 340,000 people—it offers a remarkable number of things for tourists to do.

In addition to the many activities that New Orleans provides for visitors, there is a festive quality to the city in the evenings, when people fill the music clubs in the French Quarter. You can hear music from the numerous bands in the bars, and people wander around Bourbon Street, from bar to bar, with their drinks in hand. When I visited New Orleans, I was astounded to see the way people walked around in the streets, holding their drinks.

It is a city where the celebration of the Mardi Gras is a major event in the lives of its citizens and where the carnivalization thesis of M.M. Bakhtin is operative and evident, but in a different way from Las Vegas. In part, that is because New Orleans is not a gambling centered destination (though it has lots of casinos) the way Las Vegas is. The French Quarter in New Orleans offers us images of an older and more refined America than Las Vegas does, with all its gigantic neon signs and its postmodern hotels.

Semiotically speaking, Las Vegas is pure postmodern simulation—full of gigantic, overwhelming flashing signs and huge hotels. In the French Quarter of New Orleans, on the other hand, we find an example of French architecture that was built by French immigrants in New Orleans. Many tourists find this architecture pleasant to be around and "charming," which helps explain why the French Quarter is so popular.

It is useful to think about tourism in New Orleans in terms of the various theories elaborated by scholars over the years. In his article "Marketing Mardi Gras: Commodification, Spectacle and the Political Economy of Tourism in New Orleans" Kevin Fox Gotham discusses a number of theories about tourism:

> A number of scholars have developed typologies of tourism and theories of tourist experience, and have examined the role of culture in marketing tourism among other concerns. One can find conceptions

> of tourism as a sacred crusade, pilgrimage or search for authenticity...a form of leisure and performative identity for the post-modern consumer...a form of colonialism, conquest and imperialism...a type of relation...an acculturation process...a force for historical and cultural commodification...a form of migration...and so on. Interestingly, some condemn tourism for promoting inauthentic cultural representations and distorting history...while others celebrate tourism as a mechanism to combat ethnocentrism and to foster an appreciation of different and diverse cultures. (2002:1736)

The title of Gotham's article suggests that he looks at tourism in New Orleans with a critical eye and focuses his attention on the way the Mardi Gras celebration, which started in 1857 as a celebration by local citizens, has been commodified, monetized, and used by multinational corporations for marketing purposes.

He offers an example of the Bacardi Rum campaign for "Bacardi Gras." For Gotham, New Orleans has been turned into a kind of urban theme park, and now exists as an inauthentic site for entertainment and dining by tourists. His New Orleans brings to mind Disney theme parks, but New Orleans is meant for adults, not children. Gotham mentions the work of Guy Debord and finds Debord's theories about spectacle can be applied to the New Orleans experience easily and aptly. Of course the tourists who come to New Orleans to have fun, and perhaps to enjoy the wild "anything-goes" ambience during Mardi Gras (which is a period of sexual license that would make Bakhtin's heart glad) don't have any concern with inauthenticity and matters like that. As Erik Cohen has explained, post-modern tourists aren't interested in authenticity. They just want to have a good time.

In my discussion of Las Vegas, I classified cities as being dominated by Id, Ego or Superego forces. New Orleans is definitely an "Id" city where desire and the carnal appetites are dominant, but in a more restrained and less flamboyant way than Las Vegas. For some people, New Orleans is a symbol of hedonism and excess, where alcohol flows freely and there is an ambience of sexual license and pleasure. Most of the inhabitants of New Orleans are black, but the popular image of New Orleans is French and white.

New Orleans is also the city that suffered greatly from the ravages of Hurricane Katrina, which inundated 80 percent of the city. The destruction of New Orleans by Hurricane Katrina is considered the greatest civil engineering catastrophe in American history, as the levees that were built to protect the city proved to be totally inadequate. The poor response of the Bush administration to Hurricane Katrina was also a devastating blow to President Bush's reputation and created an image of Bush as uncaring and incompetent—an image that he never was able to reverse. Part of the problem was that Bush politicized FEMA (the Federal Emergency Management Agency), the government agency that is responsible for emergencies, so it was incapable of offering an adequate response to Hurricane Katrina. So, in addition to its iconic status as a city with wonderful restaurants, a lively nightlife, and appealing architecture, New Orleans has also become a symbol of the inefficiency of the national government and of the Bush administration.

The people who suffered most were the black inhabitants of the city who lived in the low lying areas of the city. The disaster has been commodified and now there are tours of the Ninth Ward for tourists who come to party in New Orleans. New Orleans is now a destination for disaster tourists as well as fun-loving tourists.

It is one of those ironies of history that one of America's most beautiful and precious cities was devastated by one of the worst hurricanes to ever strike any city in the United States, though Hurricane Katrina also devastated many other areas near New Orleans as well. Around 1,500 people died in New Orleans as a result of the hurricane and much of the population, that was evacuated before Hurricane Katrina struck, still hasn't returned to the city. Despite the devastation, which fortunately wasn't all pervasive, New Orleans is slowly rebuilding and carries on. As a humorous bumper sticker about the city reads, "New Orleans: Third World and Proud of It!"

Chapter 25

Santa Fe, New Mexico

Located at 7,000 feet in the southern Rocky Mountains, Santa Fe is the capital of New Mexico and is one of the great destination cities of the world. The rich multicultural history, vibrant art market and active outdoor scene make for an unparalleled quality of life, and the healthy, diverse economy with low unemployment attracts entrepreneurs from all parts of the globe. There are numerous Art Galleries and Museums in Santa Fe, and culinary enthusiasts can find great Restaurants in every price range.

Santa Fe Chamber of Commerce Website

The town itself is just too rich and pretty for words. It is the oldest continuously inhabited city in America—it was founded in 1610, a decade before the Pilgrims set off from Plymouth—and takes great pride in its age. Everything in Santa Fe, and I mean everything, is made out of adobe. There's an adobe Woolworth's, an above ground multistory parking lot, an adobe six-story hotel. When you pass your first adobe gas station and adobe supermarket you think, "Hey, let's get out of here," but then you realize that it isn't something laid on for the tourists. Adobe is simply the indigenous building material, and using it everywhere gives the town a uniformity and appearance few other places achieve.... The Heart of Santa Fe is the Plaza, a Spanish-style square with white benches and a tall obelisk commemorating the battle of Valverde.

Bill Bryson, *The Lost Continent: Travels in Small Town America*

I went to Santa Fe many years ago because my brother Jason, an artist, was having a show there. I hadn't realized it but Santa Fe, a small city of around 70,000 people, is considered to be one of the two or three most important art markets in the United States after New York City. The city has countless art galleries that are supported by the tourists who visit Santa Fe and by the wealth of the people who live in and around Santa Fe.

In 1912 the city fathers decided that Santa Fe needed to find a way to distinguish itself from other cities if it was to become a major tourist destination; they saw tourism as the only way the city could flourish. The city fathers chose the Spanish Pueblo Revival look, which explains why all the buildings in Santa Fe are stucco and look, more or less, the same. The Santa Fe look is one of the most distinctive and successful examples of the way town planners can construct an identity for a town or a historic district. Planners fix upon a certain time period for their "old town" districts (often when most of the buildings in them were built) and try to give each district a "look" that is meant to appeal to tourists. Tourists like the architecture, the spatiality, and the look one finds in an "old town." These old towns feed upon the nostalgia people have for small town America and the so-called "good old days."

In 1958, the city of Santa Fe passed an ordinance that required all new and remodeled houses to have the pueblo look. The problem with having all buildings with the same style is that one gets a sense that there's something artificial and contrived about Santa Fe, that it's too precious for its own good. There is what we might call a "sham" quality of Santa Fe that caught travel writer Jan Morris's attention. She devoted a chapter on Santa Fe titled "Capital of the Holy Faith" in her book *Journeys*. Morris is one of the most important contemporary travel writers and has a superb ability to capture the ambiance of the places she visits. She was repelled by the "cute" quality of Santa Fe and wrote (1984:146–147):

> Santa Fe is the artiest, sculpturest, weaviest and potteryest town on earth, and accordingly thick with trivial parasites. There are shops with trivial names, like Tidbits or Eclectibles.... Santa Fe is infested with poseurs, old fools dressed up like Wild Bill Hickock or presiding over chichi eating-houses, young fools still living with flutes, cut-off jeans and pigtails, the vanished world of the hippies and the love-people.

She noticed that condominiums were spreading in the foothills and that the character of the city was undergoing subtle changes, as people from all over the world were attracted to living in Santa Fe.

25. *Santa Fe, New Mexico*

Santa Fe has the oldest church, the oldest government building and the oldest house in the United States. All the businesses and buildings have the same style, a harmonious look which at first sight seems quite agreeable, but for Jan Morris (145), "It is nearly all sham, though. Santa Fe's adobe is mostly less than mud-deep, being merely a cosmetic veneer over wood and concrete." She found the suburbs full of mock-adobe, tacky, and unpleasant homes and "gimcrack" shops.

Morris suggested that the area is so beautiful that it can't be completely ruined by the forces of American consumer culture and, as she puts it, can't be "overwhelmed by pretense," even though Santa Fe has more than its share of fakes and the city is succumbing to the blandishments of American culture. She wrote her article about Santa Fe in the early 1980s; it would be interesting to see what she might make of contemporary Santa Fe.

If you want to see real Hispanic culture, you can find it in California and Texas and all over the cities and towns in the American southwest, but, as if often the case, tourists prefer sanitized versions of what they are looking for rather than authenticity. If you look at a largely Hispanic town like Salinas, California, you can see the difference. Salinas has a mixture of different kinds of architecture, with many stores that cater to its large Hispanic population, including a large Mi Pueblo supermarket, and doesn't have a tailored "look" like Santa Fe.

Jean Baudrillard, who loved the American desert, might find Santa Fe interesting as an exemplar of a simulated Spanish city, designed for tourists and catering to wealthy and arty types, many of whom have second or third or fourth homes there. It can be seen, in a sense, as a themed entertainment park/city, designed for tourists who don't care very much about authenticity. The faux-adobe that one finds in Santa Fe is good enough for them.

A Conde-Nast survey found Santa Fe the ninth best city in the United States for food and wine and tenth for culture and sight-seeing. It has a dozen golf courses in the area, an opera, and many museums and historic sites. Santa Fe can be seen, if one wishes to be uncharitable, as a kind of upscale Disneyland without Mickey Mouse but with its own collection of strange characters.

A walk through San Francisco's Chinatown reveals a vibrant community with residences stacked atop commercial storefronts and parks populated with people who consider the open spaces their living rooms. They are characteristics the city's densest neighborhood has become known for worldwide.... Over the past two decades, Chinatown's population has become increasingly elderly ... The absence of families puts it at risk of being more of a tourist attraction than a living historical community.

Jessica Kwong, "Chinatown Visionary to Retire," *San Francisco Chronicle*

Chapter 26

The San Francisco Chinatown

San Francisco has the distinction of having the largest Chinatown in any non-Asian country and the oldest Chinatown in North America. It is one of San Francisco's main cultural attractions, and is generally full of tourists strolling along its two main thoroughfares, Grant Avenue and Stockton Street, window shopping and dining in one of the hundreds of Chinese restaurants that are scattered all through Chinatown. There are more than 200 restaurants in Chinatown listed in www.ChinatownSanFrancisco.com, and there are many others that are not on that list. I've seen estimates of 300 restaurants in Chinatown, and as Chinese Americans have moved to other sections of San Francisco, such as the Richmond District, there are countless other Chinese restaurants on Clement Street and Geary Avenue and many other locations in the city.

There are around 100,000 people living in Chinatown, an area of a little more than a square mile, making it the most densely populated section of the city. Many of the people who live there live below the poverty level, crowded into tiny rooms, so Chinatown can also be considered a slum. We may say that Chinatown started developing as an ethnic enclave around 1850 when Chinese immigrants, who had worked on the transcontinental railroads and participated in the Gold Rush, moved to San Francisco. When the original Chinatown burned down as a result of the 1906 earthquake and fires, it was rebuilt with buildings having faux Chinese style architecture so it would serve as a tourist attraction. And it has been an important tourist attraction for many years, since it is located just a few blocks from downtown San Francisco, within easy walking distance of Union Square.

Chinatown is one of the main attractions for tourists who come to San Francisco and want to see all the important tourist sites. Like other ethnic enclaves, there are really two Chinatowns: there is the Chinese Chinatown, which involves the life of the Chinese community living there, and there is the tourist Chinatown, which is full of tourists wandering around the district. Now, as young families leave Chinatown for other parts of the city or the suburbs, Chinatown is losing some of its vibrancy.

The original settlers of Chinatown created a number of community services, such as hospitals and social organizations to help protect people living in Chinatown. One of the most important new organizations, The Chinatown Community Development Center, created in 1977, has played a major role in shaping the social and economic life of the inhabitants of Chinatown and the city, itself, in recent decades. As a symbol of the success of the Chinese in San Francisco, the current mayor is—for the first time in history—a Chinese-American: Edward M. Lee. (By coincidence, the mayor of Oakland, just across the bay from San Francisco, is also a Chinese-American.)

There is a logical reason that ethnic and racial enclaves like Chinatown come into existence. In Chinatown, for example, there are many people who speak Chinese, there are stores that sell Chinese foodstuffs and Chinese products, there are Chinese restaurants, and there are community organizations that one can join that focus on the well-being of Chinese people in San Francisco. "Birds of a feather flock together," we say—and for a very good reason—self protection and self development. In recent decades, as Chinese Americans have become better educated and more affluent, many Chinese families have left Chinatown and moved to other districts in or near San Francisco or to the suburbs.

Geoffrey Gorer, a British anthropologist, deals with a curious aspect of American culture as it relates to Chinese immigrants. In his book *The American People: A Study in National Character,* he argues that Americans place enormous importance on how people look, which means that people of color, of all kinds, tend to be looked at with suspicion unless they show evidence of becoming "Americanized." As he writes (1964:222):

> For those countries in which the people's appearance, clothes, food, housing amenities, and political forms are completely different from those of Americans, above all the countries of Asia, the best means by which their inhabitants can be presented as tending toward Americanism, and therefore meriting treatment as human beings, is by describing their character as typically American. In recent years the Chinese have been the special recipients of this peculiar form of flattery.

He points out that Chinese immigrants turned their children into Americans so well that they were no different from EuroAmericans except in one way—their skin was yellow.

Although these American born Chinese became completely American, they still suffered when looking for jobs because, as Gorer wrote (1964:200), "Their appearance damned them; in almost any competition they were handicapped; their possibilities of employment in any mixed profession were always limited; entirely because they did not look American, they were denied full American, and therefore full human, status." Fortunately, things have changed in the years since Gorer wrote his book, and now Chinese Americans are among the most successful ethnic groups in America.

The 2010 Census reveals that America is now a multi-ethnic nation, with large numbers of people of color and many different ethnic and racial groups. One of our founding fathers, John Jay, never anticipated American becoming a multi-ethnic, multi-racial society. In a discussion of ethnicity in America, "Immigration and Ethnicity," Berndt Ostendorf and Stephan Palmié write about John Jay's hopes for a "unified" American society:

> In 1787, John Jay summed up the prospects for an American state in the *Federalist Papers.* The Americans, he argued, were a people "descended from the same ancestors, speaking the same language, professing the same religion, attached to the same principles of government, very similar in their manners and customs. Though Jay's description was already a bit of a myth in 1787—after all there were at least 200,000 Germans and Scotch-Irish, some Sephardic Jews, quite a number of Catholics and a sprinkling of Huguenots in the colonies, not to speak of the continent's aboriginal inhabitants and a sizeable number of African slaves and free blacks—it was way off the mark as a prediction of things to come. Between 1815 and 1980 approximately 46 million people from all corners of the world crossed the seas to settle in the United States and to turn it into a multicultural opposite of Jay's dream. (1993:142)

If Jay were alive now he would be astounded at the changes that have taken place in the United States as far as the racial and ethnic makeup of the American population is concerned—and the roles different ethnic groups play in American society.

One of the challenges America faces now is learning how to live with different ethnic and racial groups, and finding ways to accommodate and integrate people with different cultural beliefs and practices into American life. As the process of assimilation into American life continues, American Born Chinese (ABC's as they call themselves) face the problem of both maintaining their cultural Chinese identities and also being "typical" Americans.

Let me offer an example of Chinese-American identity loss. I showed a middle-aged Chinese American woman who works as a trainer at my gym a Chinese book cover and asked if she could translate the title. "Sorry," she said, "I don't read Chinese." "I'm a banana!" she added. "I'm yellow on the outside, but I'm white inside." I would suggest that she is somewhat unusual in that many American Born Chinese know Chinese and often converse with their friends in Chinese. But she represents a negative kind of result of the assimilation process. Racists and nativists, of course, don't care about her being "white" on the inside; it is being yellow on the outside that is the problem for them.

We used to talk about America in terms of its being a "melting pot." What has happened is that our different racial, religious, and ethnic groups have tended to live in certain enclaves— Hasidic Jews in Brooklyn, Iranians near Los Angeles, African Americans in Harlem, Vietnamese in San Jose, and Chinese in San Francisco's Chinatown.

Chapter 27

The World Trade Center

And was the bombing of the WTC with regard to the Hollywood catastrophe movies not like the snuff pornography versus ordinary sado-maso porno movies? This is the element of truth in Karl-Heinz Stockhausen's provocative statement that the planes hitting the WTC towers was the ultimate work of art: one can effectively perceive the collapse of the WTC towers as the climactic conclusion of the XXth century art's "passion of the real"—the "terrorists" themselves did not do it primarily to provoke real material damage, but FOR THE SPECTACULAR EFFECT OF IT.

www.Zizek_Welcome_to_the_Desert

Strong national symbols such as the eagle and the flag are liberally in use in the popular and mass media as a means of gathering together the imagined national community, and to these patriotic and sentimental images the twin towers of the World Trade Center have been added.... Symbols resist individualistic interpretation because they are overdetermined by customary usage, embedded so frequently in conventional discourse that they rarely take on a reflective individual meaning.

Charles H. Hill and Marguerite H. Helmers, *Defining Visual Rhetorics*

Construction work on the buildings in the World Trade Center began in 1966 and was completed between 1970 and 1973. Some thirty years after they were built, the two towers in the World Trade Center were destroyed by terrorists flying airplanes into them on September 11, 2001, a catastrophe that millions of people watched, horror-stricken, on their television sets.

After a considerable amount of wrangling between the owner of the World Trade Center and the New York Port Authority, the World Trade Center is now being rebuilt. The two towers of the World Trade Center were 1,368 and 1,362 feet high, but the new tower will be 1776 feet high—a number that ties the main tower directly to the founding of the country in 1776.

Semiotically speaking, the empty space in the New York skyline where the two towers were built is a powerful signifier of the destruction of the towers and the death of more than 3,000 people. One aspect of semiotic theory involves what we might describe as absent signs having a signifying power. That is, no sign or an absent sign can generate meaning and function as a sign. For example, not responding to a greeting conveys a message even though nothing is done. It is what was not done that conveys the message.

After almost thirty years of seeing the towers, their destruction, the empty space in the New York skyline where the towers used to be, conveyed a powerful message—one that changed America's previous sense of invulnerability and one that generated a widespread feeling of anxiety about "sleeper terrorist cells" and other menacing groups that posed a threat to the country.

The fact that we are rebuilding towers where the old towers existed and building a higher tower can be seen as a symbol of American determination. We refuse to be intimidated by the terrorist attack and are bouncing back from the tragedy of the destruction of the two towers much the same way that the people of New Orleans refused to let the destruction of many sections of the city by Hurricane Katrina keep them from rebuilding.

It took eight months to clean up the debris from the destruction of the towers and a number of years before the beginning of construction of the new tower and the complex of buildings that will form the new World Trade Center. The destruction of the towers can be seen, as Zizek points out, as a fantastic and horrific kind of media spectacular, except that it was a real event and not a simulation. Many people who saw the first plane crash into the first tower thought they were seeing some kind of television program because the notion of crashing a plane into a tower was so far-fetched. Or so it seemed. The two towers that were destroyed have been turned, as Hill and Helmers point out in the epigraph, into into a national patriotic symbol, much like the Alamo in Texas.

The rubble from the giant buildings became a magnet for disaster tourists and others curious about the scope of the disaster and about how it was being dealt with. Some tourists who visited the site, while the cleanup was going on, were motivated by curiosity and others by patriotism and many by both. These visitors wanted to see, with their own eyes, what had happened to the buildings, as if to reassure themselves that the destruction of the towers, which was replayed over and over again on television, actually happened.

In addition to its psychological impact, the destruction of the towers was a blow to our economy, as it costs billions of dollars to cart away the rubble and build a new World Trade Center. When they were built, the two towers were the tallest buildings in the world, but that distinction only lasted a year. The buildings collapsed because of the particular design of their construction; buildings built in a different way might well have survived such a crash. Skyscrapers everywhere now are designed by architects and structural engineers to withstand being attacked by planes.

The first new building to rise at the 9/11 site was 7 World Trade Center which opened in May 2006. When the rebuilding at the site of the World Trade Center is completed, there will be a number of office buildings, including a memorial to the victims of the disaster along with the 1776 foot high tower.

The area where the World Trade Center was, until the earthquake and tsunami in Japan destroyed many cities and towns and damaged four nuclear reactors, was the most important site of interest to disaster tourists. The destruction of the World Trade Center is still the most significant example of a terrorist attack that the world has seen and remains as a signifier of fanaticism in the consciousness of everyone who has seen images of the planes hitting the two towers and then of their collapse into a gigantic pile of rubble.

References

Bakhtin, Mikhail M. 1984.
Trans. Hélène Iswolsky.
Rabelais and His World.
Bloomington: Indiana University Press.

Barthes, Roland, 1979.
Trans. Richard Howard.
The Eiffel Tower and Other Mythologies.
New York: Hill & Wang.

Baudrillard, Jean. 1996.
"Disneyworld Company."
Trans. Francois Debrix.
Liberation, March 4.

Baudrillard, Jean.
"The Precession of Simulacra."
In *Simulacra and Simulation.* 1981/1994.
Ann Arbor: University of Michigan Press.

Baudrillard, Jean. 1970/1998.
The Consumer Society: Myths & Structures.
Thousand Oaks, CA: Sage Publications.

Berger, Arthur Asa. 2005.
Media Analysis Techniques. 4th Edition.
Thousand Oaks, CA: Sage Publications.

Brear, Holly. 1995.
Inherit the Alamo: Myth and Ritual at an American Shrine.
Austin: University of Texas Press.

Brody, Michael. 1976.
"The Wonderful World of Disney:
Its Psychological Appeal."
American Imago 33: 350–360.

Brooker, William. 1999.
Cultural Theory: A Glossary.
London: Arnold.

Brush, Molly. 2005.
"Royal Hawaiian Dance: How Hotels Commodified the Hula."
Thesis, Senior Seminar in Dance, Barnard College.

Bryson, Bill. 1990.
The Lost Continent: Travels in Small-Town America.
New York: Harper Perennial.

Chambers, Erve. Ed. 1997.
Tourism and Culture: An Applied Perspective.
New York: State University of New York Press.

Cohen, Erik. 2008.
"The Changing Face of Contemporary Tourism."
Society 5 (4): 330–333.

Danesi, Marcel. 2008.
Why It Sells: Decoding the Meaning of Brand Names, Logos, Ads, and Other Marketing and Advertising Ploys.
Lanham, MD: Rowman & Littlefield.

Debord, Guy. 1995.
The Society of the Spectacle.
Brooklyn, NY: Zone Books.

de Saussure, Ferdinand. 1915/1966. Trans. W. Baskin.
Course in General Linguistics.
New York: McGraw-Hill.

de Toqueville, Alexis. 1956.
Democracy in America.
New York: Mentor Books.

Eliade, Mircea. 1961.
The Sacred and the Profane: The Nature of Religion.
New York: Harvest Books.

Emerson, Ralph W.
In Norman Foerster, Ed. 1957. *American Poetry and Prose.* 4th Edition.
Boston: Houghton Mifflin

Flores, Richard. 2002.
Remembering the Alamo: Memory, Modernity and Master Symbol.
Austin: University of Texas Press.

Freud, Sigmund.
In *A General Introduction to Psychoanalysis.* 1953.
New York: Permabooks.

Freud, Sigmund.
In *Character and Culture.* Philip Rieff, Ed. 1963.
New York: Collier Books.

Gabriel, Ralph Henry. 1956.
The Course of American Democratic Thought. 2nd Edition.
New York: Ronald Press.

Geertz, Clifford. 1973.
The Interpretation of Cultures: Selected Essays.
New York: Basic Books.

Gilbert, Martin. 2007.
"Mad Men."
Boston Globe. July 12.

Gorer, Geoffrey. 1964.
The American People: A Study in National Character.
New York: W.W. Norton.

Gotham, Kevin Fox. 2002.
"Marketing Mardi Gras: Commodification, Spectacle and the Political Economics of Tourism in New Orleans."
Urban Studies 39 (10): 1735.

Gottdiener, Mark. 1982.
"Disneyland: A Utopian Urban Space,"
Journal of Contemporary Ethnography 11(2): 139.

Gottdiener, Mark. 1996.
The Theming of America: Dreams, Visions and Commercial Spaces.
Boulder, CO: Westview Press.
Haug, Wolfgang. 1971. Trans. Robert Bock.
Critique of Commodity Aesthetics; Appearance, Sexuality and Advertising in Capitalist Society
Minneapolis: University of Minnesota Press.

Henderson, Joseph L.
"Ancient Myths and Modern Man."
In Carl G. Jung. 1968. *Man and His Symbols.*
New York: Laurel Books.

Henniger, Daniel. 2003.
"Mall of America: Still Home for Shop 'til You Drop."
Wall Street Journal. October 3.

Jameson, Fredric. 1991.
Postmodernism or, The Cultural Logic of Late Capitalism.
Durham, NC: Duke University Press.

Lathan, Ralph. 2009.
"Celebrities and Substance Abuse."
Baylor University Medical Proceedings. October.

Lefebvre, Henri. 1971. Trans. Sacha Rabinovitch.
Everyday Life in the Modern World.
New York: Harper & Row.

Lipset, Seymour Martin.
The First New Nation: The United States in Historical and Comparative Perspective.
New York: W.W. Norton.

Lyotard, Jean-François. 1984. Trans. G. Bennington and B. Massumi.
The Postmodern Condition: A Report on Knowledge.
Minneapolis: University of Minnesota Press.

MacCannell, Dean. 1976.
The Tourist: A New Theory of The Leisure Class
New York: Schocken Books.
Marcus, Greil. 1982.
Mystery Train: Images of America in Rock 'n 'Roll Music. Revised Edition.
New York: E. P. Dutton.

McLuhan, Marshall. 1951.
The Mechanical Bride: The Folklore of Industrial Man.
Boston: Beacon Press.

Mehrhoff, W. Arthur. 1992.
The Gateway Arch: Fact & Symbol.
Bowling Green, OH: Bowling Green State University Popular Press.

Morgan, Diane.
"Postmodernism and Architecture." In Stuart Sim, Ed.
The Routledge Companion to Postmodernism. 2005.
New York: Routledge.

Morris, Jan. 1984.
Journeys.
New York: Oxford Books

Morris, Jan. 1982.
Destinations: Essays from Rolling Stone.
New York: Oxford University Press,

Morton, Cole. 2010.
"First Person" Interview with Dick Zigun.
The Financial Times. October 9/10.

Neumann, Mark. 1999.
On the Rim: Looking for the Grand Canyon.
Minneapolis: University of Minnesota Press.

Ostendorf, Berndt and Stephan Palmié.
In M.G. Gidley, Ed. 1993. *Modern American Culture: An Introduction.*
London: Longman.

Peirce, Charles S.
Epigraph.
In T. Sebeok. 1977. *A Perfusion of Signs.*
Bloomington: Indiana University Press.

Persons, Stow. 1958.
American Minds: A History of Ideas.
New York: Henry Holt & Company.

Pines, Maya. 1982.
"How They Know What You Really Mean"
San Francisco Chronicle. October 13.

Powdermaker, Hortense. 1951.
Hollywood, the Dream Factory: an Anthropologist Looks at the Movie Makers.
Boston: Little, Brown.

Pretes, Michael.
In E. Chambers, Ed. 1997. *Tourism and Culture: An Applied Perspective.*
New York: State University of New York Press.

Pretes, Michael. 2003.
"Tourism and Nationalism."
The Annals of Tourism Research 30 (1): 125.

Rogers, Richard and Julia Kalil Schuten. 2004.
"The Gender of Water and the Pleasures of Alienation: A Critical Analysis of Visiting Hoover Dam."
The Communication Review 7: 259.

Ross, Ralph. 1962.
Symbols and Civilization.
New York: Harbinger Books.

Schickel, Richard. 1968.
The Disney Version.
New York: Avon Books.

Simmel, Georg.
In Donald N. Levine, Ed. 1971. *On Individuality and Social Forms: Selected Writings.*
Chicago: University of Chicago Press.

Solomon, Jack. 1990.
The Signs of Our Time: The Secret Meanings of Everyday Life.
New York: Harper & Row.

Thompson, Michael, Richard Ellis and Aaron Wildavsky. 1990.
Cultural Theory.
Boulder, CO; Westview.

Turner, Frederick Jackson. 1893.
"The Significance of the Frontier in American History."
Paper presented to the American Historical Society.

Venturi, Robert, Steven Izenour, and Denise Scott Brown. 1977.
Learning from Las Vegas. Revised Edition.
Cambridge, MA: MIT Press.

Ward, David A. and Thomas G. Werlich. 2003.
"Alcatraz and Marion: Evaluating Super-Maximum Custody."
Personality and Society 3(5): 53.

Wildavsky, Aaron B.
"Choosing Preferences by Constructing Institutions: A Cultural Theory of Preference Formation."
In Arthur A. Berger, Ed. 1989. *Political Culture and Public Opinion.*
New Brunswick, NJ: Transaction.

Williams, Raymond. 1977.
Marxism and Literature.
Oxford: Oxford University Press.

Zeyman, Jay J.
"Peirce's Theory of Signs,"
In T.S. Sebeok, Ed. 1977. *A Perfusion of Signs.*
Bloomington: Indiana University Press.

Zukin, Sharon. 2005.
Point of Purchase: How Shopping Changed American Culture.
New York: Routledge.

Index

Index

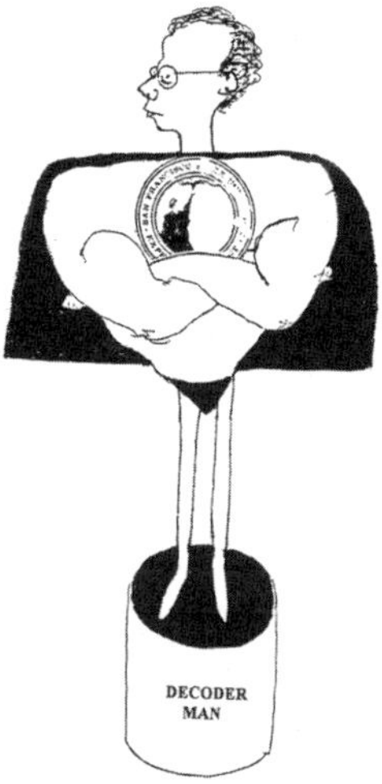

About the Author

Arthur Asa Berger is professor emeritus of Broadcast and Electronic Communication Arts at San Francisco State University, where he taught between 1965 and 2003. He graduated in 1954 from the University of Massachusetts in Amherst, Massachusetts; he majored in Literature and minored in Philosophy and Art. He received a Master's Degree in Journalism (but also studied at the Writers Workshop) from the University of Iowa in 1956 and was elected to the University of Iowa School of Journalism and Mass Communication's "Hall of Fame" in 2009. He received a Ph.D. in American Studies from the University of Minnesota in 1965. He wrote his dissertation on the comic strip *Li'l Abner.*

In 1963 he had a Fulbright scholarship to Italy, and in 1983–84 was visiting professor at the Annenberg School for Communication at the University of Southern California. He has also taught at Heinrich Heine University in Dusseldorf, Germany, at Hong Kong Polytechnic University in Hong Kong, and in China at Jinan University in Guangzhou and Tsinghua University in Beijing. Over the years he has lectured in more than a dozen countries such as England, Denmark, Norway, Sweden, Finland, France, Germany, Italy, Turkey, Tunisia, Morocco, Russia and Ukraine.

He has published more than one hundred articles in publications such as *The Journal of Communication, Society, Rolling Stone,* the *San Francisco Chronicle* and the *Los Angeles Times,* and more than sixty books on media, popular culture, humor, and tourism. Among his books are: *Signs in Contemporary Culture: An Introduction to Semiotics; Seeing is Believing: An Introduction to Visual Communication; What Objects Mean: An Introduction to Material Culture; Media and Society; Media and Communication Research Methods; Making Sense of Media; Bloom's Morning; Ads, Fads and Consumer Culture;* and *Shop 'Til You Drop.* His work has focused on the impact of media and popular culture on individuals and on American consumer culture. He has also written a number of academic murder mysteries such as *Postmortem for a Postmodernist, The Mass Comm Murders: Five Media Theorists Self-Destruct,* and *Durkheim is Dead: Sherlock Holmes is Introduced to Sociological Theory.*

Dr. Berger is married and has two children and four grandchildren. He lives in Mill Valley, California, and enjoys foreign travel and dining in ethnic restaurants. He can be reached at: arthurasaberger@gmail.com.